LIVING PURE INSIDE OUT

BILL HUGHES

LifeWay Press
Nashville, Tennessee

ISBN 0-6330-8006-3

This book is a resource in the "Ethics" category
of the Christian Growth Study Plan.
Course CG-0803
Dewey Decimal Classification: 306.73
Subject Heading: SEXUAL ABSTINENCE \ SEXUAL BEHAVIOR

Student Ministry Publishing
LifeWay Church Resources
One LifeWay Plaza
Nashville, TN 37234-0174

Printed in the United States of America.
To order additional copies of this resource: WRITE LifeWay Church Resources Customer
Service, One LifeWay Plaza, Nashville, TN 37234-0113; FAX order to (615) 251-5933;
PHONE 1-800-458-2772; E-MAIL to CustomerService@lifeway.com; ONLINE at
www.lifeway.com; or visit the LifeWay Christian Store serving you.

We believe that the Bible has God for its author; salvation for its end;
and truth, without any mixture of error, for its matter and that all Scripture is totally true and
trustworthy. The 2000 statement of
The Baptist Faith and Message is our doctrinal guideline.

CONTENTS

SESSION 1: PURITY...IT'S A GOD THING 6

SESSION 2: I CAN'T...BUT HE CAN 19

SESSION 3: SECRET SIN 34

SESSION 4: LIVING IN PURITY 50

SESSION 5: MAKING A COMMITMENT TO PURITY 65

LEADER GUIDE 78

ABOUT THE AUTHOR

Bill Hughes lives in Tifton, Georgia, with his wife Dana, a middle school teacher and part time missionary to China, and two teenage daughters. He has been a youth minister for 29 years, the last 12 years at First Baptist Church in Tifton. He graduated from the University of Central Florida, where he played soccer, and The Southern Baptist Theological Seminary. In his spare time Bill plays golf, runs, and at the age of 49 still plays in an adult flag football league.

HOW THIS BOOK WORKS

In 1994, teenagers from all over America gathered on the mall in Washington, D.C. Their purpose was to tell the nation that Christian teenagers were taking a stand for sexual purity. The mall was covered with plastic holders, each containing a pledge from a teenager to remain sexually abstinent until marriage. The nation took notice and the True Love Waits movement was born. The rate of teen pregnancies began to decline. There was a drop in the number of teen abortions. Most of all, God was honored by the commitment of teenagers to Him.

Perhaps you have studied other True Love Waits books. You may have signed a True Love Waits pledge and participated in a worship service where you made a vow of purity. If so, this book is for you. It will help you to live out the commitments you have made.

Perhaps this is the first time you have heard about True Love Waits. Waiting until marriage to have sex may seem totally unrealistic to you. You may not even know why you are reading this material. Well, don't worry. This book will give you a chance to truly understand what it means to live a pure life. Our hope is that after you have finished this study, you will have a better understanding of who you are, why saving sex for marriage is important, and where to get the power to wait.

This book can be used in a variety of ways. It contains five in-depth Bible studies that focus on purity. You can work through this material on your own, with your parents, in a group with parents and youth, or in a small "peer" discipleship group. These sessions also can be used for group Bible study sessions at retreats or DiscipleNow weekends. You can even take this material to school and lead a study in a Christian club. If possible, include your parents in your study of *Living Pure Inside Out*. You may be amazed at how it will improve your relationship with them. Plus, they may just learn something from you.

The Bible studies are designed to be interactive. You don't just read; you get involved. Sometimes you will write your response to a question in the space below it. Some questions have one answer and you are to check the correct box. Other questions will have more than one correct answer, and you will be instructed to check two or more boxes. When you find fill-in-the-blank spaces, the first letter to the correct answer will be given. If the fill-in-the-blank is part of a Bible verse, the answer has been based on the *New Living Translation.* When you see "Point to Ponder," highlight that paragraph. There is one "Point to Ponder" in each Bible study which gives the main point of that study. So ponder it! The final part of each Bible study is titled "True Love Waits." This part summarizes the Bible study and ties the five studies together. At the end of each study is a closing prayer. Pray this prayer aloud if it expresses the desire of your heart after studying God's Word.

In the back of this book is a leader guide for teaching the five Bible studies. All the correct answers to the response questions are found in the leader guide. The leader guide is designed to be used in a small group of 6 to 12 youth or a mixed group of parents and youth. Teaching each of the Bible studies using the procedures in the leader guide will take about 60 minutes. The leader guide lists supplies you will need to enhance the learning experience. There are also optional activities listed in the leader guide which can be used for DiscipleNow weekends and retreats. Although groups can be either co-ed or same-gender groups, some of the material may be more thoroughly discussed if the groups are same-gender groups.

As you begin your study of *Living Pure Inside Out,* whether by yourself, with your parents, or with a group of friends, it is essential that you stay open to hearing God. God wants to do awesome things in your life. Are you ready to listen to Him?

Session 1

PURITY... IT'S A GOD THING

ONE: A PICTURE OF PURITY

"Let's go," Calvin told his wife of 60 years. "I'm ready for our walk."

"Just wait, old man," Sylvia responded. "I've got to get my walking shoes on." She hiked up her dress, slightly exposing one knee. The 80-year-old Calvin saw it and let out a long wolf-whistle. "Calvin, quit that," she told him. "I'm nearly 80 and you already are." But her smile told him that she secretly enjoyed his boyish attention.

Calvin and Sylvia met in high school and married after seeing each other for a year. Neither of them had ever touched another person sexually, and didn't touch each other until their wedding night. They both loved God passionately, even in their old age, and they loved each other more now than they did when they were 20. There had been some hard years, but Calvin and Sylvia had seen God do incredible things in their lives.

Katherine dried her tears as she got ready for work. She felt so lonely as she thought back over her life. She had gotten pregnant at age 18, and the guy she was dating took off when he realized she planned to keep the baby. Katherine had searched for someone else to love her and her little girl. She had married four times, but each marriage had ended with much pain. Katherine's daughter was now 18 and had moved out of the house. Empty, struggling, and alone, Katherine was still looking for her one true love.

Have you seen couples like Calvin and Sylvia? Do you know people who are still in love after a lifetime together? Chances are, you know someone like Katherine, too. You might think that Calvin was lucky and Katherine was unlucky, but there is a deeper truth. The real difference between Calvin and Katherine is not that Calvin found the right person and Katherine didn't. The real difference is that Calvin was the right person.

At an early age, Calvin chose to live a life of purity before God. It was never easy, but he was ready to honor Sylvia when God brought her into his life. He waited for God's best … but he did more than wait. He lived a pure life.

Times have changed. Living a pure life may be harder for you than it was for Calvin. Still, the call of God is the same. The rewards are the same. And the alternative of compromise and heartache is the same. The question is, are you ready to live pure?

TWO: WHAT IS PURITY?

Neither Kim nor Sam had ever had sex before they started going out. They were waiting for someone they really loved. Now they are dating exclusively and both feel like they have found true love. So they start sleeping together. Is this sexual purity?

Justin doesn't want to get his girlfriend pregnant, but doesn't see any problem with sexual activity as long as they don't actually have intercourse. Is he practicing sexual purity?

Vonda knows that she and Micah will get married someday. She does not plan to ever have sex with anyone but Micah. It seems silly to them to wait so long to have sex just because they haven't actually had the wedding ceremony. So they decide to go ahead and have sex. Are they practicing sexual purity?

Danny refuses to go too far on dates. He is careful not to touch girls in sexual ways. When Danny is alone, however, he fantasizes about the girls he dates and thinks about what it would be like to have sex with them. He figures he's OK since he isn't actually doing anything with them. Is he practicing sexual purity?

The whole concept of sexual purity may be difficult to define. Which of the following would best define sexual purity as you see it? Check one.

- ☐ **Not going "all the way" until marriage**
- ☐ **Not watching pornographic movies**
- ☐ **Not touching another person any place that a swimming suit would cover**
- ☐ **A total commitment to godliness in every area of my life**

It is true that you can't be involved in sex outside of marriage or pornography and still maintain sexual purity. Hopefully, however, you checked the last answer. Purity is more than setting a few limits in your dating life. It is more than a list of things to do and not do. It is a total commitment of your life to God. **Look up Matthew 5:8 and fill in these words of Jesus:**

"God blesses those whose h__________ are p________, for they will s_____ G______."

POINT TO PONDER

Being pure means totally offering yourself to God.

In the Old Testament, King David also wrote about total life purity. For example, look at these verses:

> Who may climb the mountain of the Lord? Who may stand in his holy place? Only those whose hands and hearts are pure, who do not worship idols and never tell lies (Ps. 24:3-4).

Some of you are probably thinking that David was talking about the great joy of mountain climbing. You guys missed the point. Mountain climbing may be fun, but David really was asking how a person can have a right relationship with God.

What was the answer?

- ☐ **Go to church all the time**
- ☐ **Be a full-time minister**
- ☐ **Have nothing to lose**
- ☐ **Have pure hands and a pure heart**

You may be saying, "That's great, but that still doesn't answer the question. How can someone *have* a pure heart?" Read the last part of these verses again. A person with pure heart does not "worship idols." An idol is something that replaces God as your object of worship. It could be a hot car, popularity, a boyfriend or girlfriend—anything that becomes more important to you than God. David also said that a person with a pure heart will "never tell lies." Purity means that you don't tie yourself to things that are contrary to God's truth. Does your life honor God, or do you have other things that are more important to you?

Purity is a lot more than abstaining from sex. It involves the way you interact with other people. It includes the things you think about. It involves how you spend your time. Real purity is a matter of having your total life committed to God.

Think about your life. How would you describe your own personal purity? Check one.

- ☐ **I don't really want my life to be committed to God.**
- ☐ **Pure heart? I wish.**
- ☐ **There are a couple of areas of my life that need some work.**
- ☐ **I mess up sometimes, but I'm definitely growing in personal purity.**

In the space below, write anything you think would need to change for you to truly have a pure heart. What would it take to change that?

THREE: A MESSED-UP WORLD

How would you describe a perfect world? Would you say it is a place where everyone loves other people? Would you say that everyone does what is right? I suspect you would say that the perfect world wouldn't include things like hatred, abuse, and pain. In a perfect world, it would be easy to live a pure life. But that's not the world we live in, is it?

We live in a messed-up world. Planes crash into buildings. Hand grenades explode in houses of worship. Children shoot other children. Something has gone terribly wrong in the world. The world has been messed up almost since the beginning. Paul talked about the kind of world we have in the following passage.

Yes, they knew God, but they wouldn't worship him as God or even give him thanks. And they began to think up foolish ideas of what God was like. The result was that their minds became dark and confused. Claiming to be wise, they became utter fools instead. And instead of worshiping the glorious, ever-living God, they worshiped idols made to look like mere people, or birds and animals and snakes. So God let them go ahead and do whatever shameful things their hearts desired. As a result, they did vile and degrading things with each other's bodies. Instead of believing what they knew was the truth about God, they deliberately chose to believe lies. So they worshiped the things God made but not the Creator himself, who is to be praised forever. Amen (Rom. 1:21-25).

These verses explain how the world became so messed up. How did things get so out of hand? Check two or more.

- ☐ **People did not know there was a God.**
- ☐ **People worshiped the creation, not the Creator.**
- ☐ **People refused to glorify or thank God.**
- ☐ **Parents made up too many rules.**
- ☐ **Sinful hearts led to sexual impurity.**

Once people started living in rebellion, things just went downhill. Paul continued in this passage.

That is why God abandoned them to their shameful desires. Even the women turned against the natural way to have sex and instead indulged in sex with each other. And the men, instead of having normal sexual relationships with women, burned with lust for each other. Men did shameful things with other men and, as a result, suffered within themselves the penalty they so richly deserved. When they refused to acknowledge God, he abandoned them to their evil minds and let them do things that should never be done (Rom. 1:26-28).

As people got worse and worse, what happened to their minds?

They became e____________ . People did things that s___________ n________ b____ d________ .

The evil minds of men meant that their behavior became evil. Paul spelled out just how evil man became.

Their lives became full of every kind of wickedness, sin, greed, hate, envy, murder, fighting, deception, malicious behavior, and gossip. They are backstabbers, haters of God, insolent, proud, and boastful. They are forever inventing new ways of sinning and are disobedient to their parents. They refuse to understand, break their promises, and are heartless and unforgiving. They are fully aware of God's death penalty for those who do these things, yet they go right ahead and do them anyway. And, worse yet, they encourage others to do them, too (Rom. 1:29-32).

Can you see the behaviors Paul described in this passage in the world around you? People have chosen to live in a way that is contrary to God's standards for them. There is no area of life where that is more evident than in the area of sexuality.

Check the statements below that sound like things you have heard people at school say. Check two or more.

- ☐ **Sex is love, and love is sex.**
- ☐ **Sex outside of marriage is OK as long as you are in love.**
- ☐ **Teenagers need to experiment with sex in order to learn about sex.**
- ☐ **Have fun, just be careful not to get pregnant.**
- ☐ **If you are dating you are supposed to have sex.**
- ☐ **Everyone is having sex.**
- ☐ **Sex shows you are mature.**
- ☐ **Only losers wait until marriage.**
- ☐ **It's only sex!**

You probably checked every statement. All of these ideas are expressed everyday on just about every campus in America. The ideas are reinforced by the stories told on television and in the movies.

In the space below, write the names of television shows or movies you have seen that send the message that sexual purity is unwanted, unnecessary, or just doesn't exist.

Imagine you are from outer space and you just landed on earth. When you get here you start watching television, maybe even some of the pay-per-view channels. You decide to check out the Internet and you start surfing by clicking on the advertisements that come up on your screen. Just from these few experiences on earth, what would you conclude about this world and its inhabitants?

FOUR: GOD'S EXPECTATION OF SEXUAL PURITY

OK, this seems impossible. We live in this messed-up world where we are constantly bombarded with evil thoughts and impure behavior. Yet we are supposed to be totally committed to godly living in every area of our life, including our sexuality. Yeah right.

Yeah, right!

As impossible as it sounds, God has called us to live in a way that is radically different than this messed-up world. In biblical times, the city of Corinth was known for lustful living. Sexual immorality was a way of life in Corinth. It was every bit as sex-saturated as the culture we live in. Still, look at what Paul wrote to them.

Run away from sexual sin! No other sin so clearly affects the body as this one does. For sexual immorality is a sin against your own body. Or don't you know that your body is the temple of the Holy Spirit, who lives in you and was given to you by God? You do not belong to yourself, for God bought you with a high price. So you must honor God with your body (1 Cor. 6:18-20).

Paul called the Christians in the city of Corinth to a different lifestyle. Why should Christians live differently from their neighbors? The key is found in these words: "You do not belong to yourself, for God bought you with a high price." What was the price?

What do you think "You do not belong to yourself" means? Check one.

- ☐ **You cannot run your own life.**
- ☐ **Your life belongs to God.**
- ☐ **Your life is not worth much.**
- ☐ **Life is not owned by anyone.**

Do you understand this incredible truth? God has the right to ask so much of us because He has already given so much to us. The price He paid was giving His own Son, Jesus, to be the sacrifice for our sins. By His death, He earned the right to call us His own.

Joey had grown up in church. He had heard all of the rules, but it just didn't connect for him. He didn't see how anyone could ever be good enough to keep all of those rules. He was at a youth camp when it finally came together. Joey realized that he could never be good enough for God; he was a sinner and had fallen short of God's law. That was why Jesus came to earth. By His death, Jesus had paid the entire price for Joey's sin. Joey could be completely forgiven because of what Jesus had done for him. Joey accepted God's gift of salvation and asked Jesus to be Lord of his life. Joey realized that he owed everything to Jesus.

If you are a Christian, your life belongs to God. God expects incredible things of those who belong to Him, including sexual purity. Jesus sacrificed so much for us that the only appropriate response for the Christian is to be obedient to God's call.

God wants you to be holy, so you should keep clear of all sexual sin. Then each of you will control your body and live in holiness and honor (1 Thess. 4:3-4).

What is God's will for you according to these verses?

There is no question about God's desire for us to be sexually pure. Below are a list of actions and activities that relate to many teens.

Check the activities that would not be holy and honorable. Check two or more.

- ☐ **Viewing movies with strong sexual content**
- ☐ **Telling dirty jokes**
- ☐ **Reading provocative and enticing books**
- ☐ **Calling a phone-sex number**
- ☐ **Looking at sexual web sites**
- ☐ **Fantasizing about a boyfriend or girlfriend**

It really is not difficult to know what is holy and honorable. If you are a Christian, the Holy Spirit will always let you know if your actions and attitudes are holy and honorable.

Write a prayer in the space below thanking Jesus for doing so much for you.

FIVE: TRUE LOVE WAITS

God has called you to a life of purity. This life requires guarding your relationships so you don't get involved in a sexual relationship until you can share it with the person you marry. But it means more than that. It means every area of your life is offered to God. The things you look at, say, listen to, and even think about are to be pure.

God has the right to ask you to live a pure life. He allowed His own Son to die for your sins. When you became a Christian, you became His. There is nothing He could ask that would be too great. And yet, everything He asks and requires of you He asks because of His great love for you.

True purity makes all the difference in life. A pure life is a life free of guilt. A pure life involves an open line of communication with the God of the universe. A pure life means healthy relationships with friends, family members, boyfriends or girlfriends, and with your future mate. A pure life means that you can be the person God intends for you to be. God does not require purity because He wants to place a difficult task on us. He requires purity because it will set us free.

Closing Prayer: *Jesus, I know You want me to be pure in every area of my life. I know that my life belongs to You, so I commit myself to Your will for my life. Thank You for loving me enough to call me to a lifestyle that will be of such great blessing to me. In Jesus name, Amen.*

Session 2

I CAN'T ... BUT HE CAN

ONE: I CAN'T

James had been dating Jennifer for several months. They both were Christians and they understood God's standard of purity. Still, their relationship was becoming more and more physical. James felt guilty about the direction their relationship was taking. Even more, he knew that if they kept going as they were, they soon would be having sex.

About that time, James' church held a True Love Waits emphasis. It seemed like perfect timing! James saw this as his way out. He signed a True Love Waits pledge card and got Jennifer to do the same. He was sure that everything would change. Now he thought he could relax with Jennifer and not worry about having sex.

Only a few weeks later, James and Jennifer ended up sleeping together. James couldn't believe that he had violated his own commitment. He felt terribly guilty. But, he also felt like God had let him down.

What happened? Why didn't James' commitment "stick"?

A lot of students have made commitments to sexual purity only to find themselves doing the very thing they promised not to do. Even students who remain sexually abstinent fail to remain truly pure. Thinking lustful thoughts, practicing masturbation, and viewing pornography are just some of the ways they let their hearts fall into impurity. Is there any hope for a pure life? Are humans merely doomed to act on their own desires?

Good news! Purity is possible. However, it requires a different approach than the one James used.

TWO: THE BIG PROBLEM

1. You inherited a sinful nature.

The big problem we have to face is that we all have inherited a sinful nature. No one has to teach us how to do things that are sinful; we know how to do that from the beginning. Here is the way Paul described it in the Bible:

When Adam sinned, sin entered the entire human race. Adam's sin brought death, so death spread to everyone, for everyone sinned. Yes, people sinned even before the law was given. And though there was no law to break, since it had not yet been given, they all died anyway—even though they did not disobey an explicit commandment of God, as Adam did. What a contrast between Adam and Christ, who was yet to come! (Rom. 5:12-14)

According to these verses, which of the following are true? Check two or more.

- ☐ **Not all people are sinners.**
- ☐ **Sin came into the world through Adam and was passed down to all people.**
- ☐ **Sin existed even when there was no set of rules to follow.**
- ☐ **Even if you don't know the rules, you are still in sin.**

Since you are born with sin, you are born impure. Even the most beautiful baby is born impure. He cannot be totally committed to God on his own. It is impossible because of who his relatives are. He is a descendant of Adam.

2. Just wanting to be pure is not enough.

Since you are studying this material, you probably have a desire to be pure. There is a tendency to think that if we desire purity and then strive for purity, we will be pure. Unfortunately, that is not the case. Even the apostle Paul admitted failure when it came to doing good.

I know I am rotten through and through so far as my old sinful nature is concerned. No matter which way I turn, I can't make myself do right. I want to, but I can't (Rom. 7:18).

What did Paul say about his desire?

In the same verse, what did Paul say about his ability to put this desire into practice?

I c________ m________ myself d____ r__________.

When I want to do good, I don't. And when I try not to do wrong, I do it anyway (Rom. 7:19).

Paul wanted more than anything to live a pure life. But what did he do? Check one.

☐What he desired
☐What was wrong
☐The best he could
☐The little things right

Paul desired to do right. He desired to be pure. He desired to live a life that reflected Jesus Christ. But what did he do? He did the opposite. He did the very things he didn't want to do. How crazy is that?

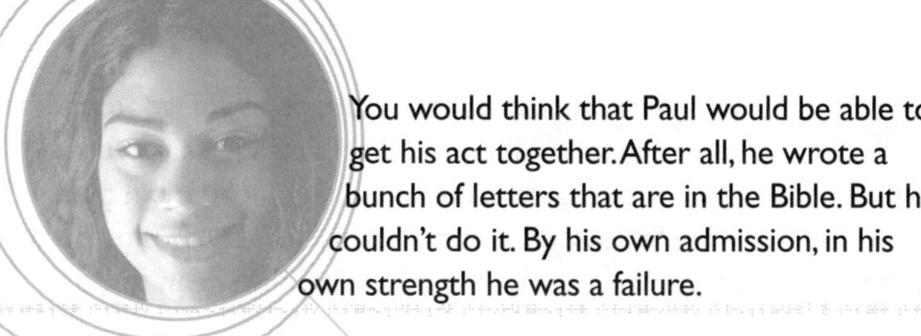

You would think that Paul would be able to get his act together. After all, he wrote a bunch of letters that are in the Bible. But he couldn't do it. By his own admission, in his own strength he was a failure.

3. God never intended us to live purely in our own strength. There is a part of us that really desires to go out and do something for God. The something we do may be witnessing, giving money, or even becoming a missionary. Teens are often drawn to live a pure life for God. Unfortunately, when these things we desire to do for God are done in our own strength, we have totally missed God's plan for us.

For we are God's masterpiece. He has created us anew in Christ Jesus, so that we can do the good things he planned for us long ago (Eph. 2:10).

According to this verse, who is God's "masterpiece"?

According to this verse, as Christians, we were created in what? Check one.

- ☐ **In Christ**
- ☐ **In our power**
- ☐ **In our image**
- ☐ **In desperation**

According to this verse, what is the result of being created in Christ? Check one.

- ☐ **Good works**
- ☐ **Unknown to man**
- ☐ **Baptism**
- ☐ **A good name**

Do you see it? God never wanted us to try and do all the good things we are constantly trying (and failing) to do, because He wants to do these good things through us. He is the one doing the work in us, not ourselves. We are in His strength not our own. He is doing through us the things He wants to do, not the things we think we need to do.

THREE: WALK IN GRACE

It was early in the morning. The school halls were still quiet, but eight teens were gathered in a classroom with their Bibles open.

"Wow," Michael said, "if the apostle Paul couldn't keep from sinning, how can I?" The group had obviously been reading Romans 7:18-19. "Those verses can sure seem depressing," Michael went on. "I guess I should just give up and forget trying to be a righteous person."

"You can't think that way," Steph told him. "Remember the little train that could? 'I think I can, I think I can, I think I can.'"

"Freshmen!" Michael grunted.

But how can we keep going if Paul couldn't even live a godly life? It would seem like Michael and Steph had the only two answers. Like Michael said you can give up and quit trying. After all, you reason, no one else is living a pure life so why should you? Or you can just try harder like Steph said … rather lamely. Just buck up, you tell yourself, and try harder! You can do it! Just don't quit!

You probably have tried both of those approaches. I have, too. You probably have discovered like I have that neither of them really work. Fortunately, Paul didn't quit writing after he talked about all of his struggles. He went on to tell us the answer. Check out these verses:

Oh, what a miserable person I am! Who will free me from this life that is dominated by sin? Thank God! The answer is in Jesus Christ our Lord. So you see how it is: In my mind I really want to obey God's law, but because of my sinful nature I am a slave to sin (Rom. 7:24-25).

What is the answer to the problem of our impurity?
☐You'll always be a slave, so just accept it.
☐Think really hard about God and you'll get over it.
☐Trust Jesus Christ to be your help.

It sounds simplistic, doesn't it? Jesus Christ is the answer. It sounds like it is just too easy, but I can promise you that it is anything but easy. **What does it mean for Jesus to be the answer?**

Purity is not just about doing the right thing. It is about being cleaned up from the inside out. That is what Jesus does. When you place your entire trust in Him, He cleanses you from all impurity. That is why Paul wrote this:

So now there is no condemnation for those who belong to Christ Jesus (Rom. 8:1).

Think of it! *No condemnation!* Have you made some mistakes that have caused you to be impure? Of course! Will you make more? If Paul is right about the whole "law of sin" thing, you can be sure that you will. But, you are not condemned!

Think of it like this: You pour a glass of pure, clean, filtered water. You hold it up to the light; it is so pure that there are no little floatie things like you usually see in tap water. It is absolutely pure water. You lick your lips, anticipating the absolutely pure water. About that time, your parakeet flies over and leaves a little present in your water. Well, that's just one little impurity. It's not like the water was taken from the sewer. So you just go ahead and drink it, right? No? Of course, you pour it out and proceed to wash the glass before you fill it with more water.

Trying harder might mean that we don't add as much impurity to our lives, but it doesn't take away the impurity we have allowed to fall there. What Jesus Christ alone can do is make the water completely pure again. In Christ, we are completely clean.

Do we just give up and quit trying? Not at all. We just start trying in a different way by trusting Christ, not our own efforts. Look at Paul's explanation:

> Those who are dominated by the sinful nature think about sinful things, but those who are controlled by the Holy Spirit think about things that please the Spirit. If your sinful nature controls your mind, there is death. But if the Holy Spirit controls your mind, there is life and peace (Rom. 8:5-6).

Jeff and his girlfriend, Susan, were at a church retreat. They were both praying for lost friends they had brought with them. They were looking forward to seeing what God would do. Some of their friends liked to tease them asking, "Why don't you guys ever go to movies together like normal couples? It seems like all of your dates are church functions."

Jeff and Susan had been to a couple of movies together, but their friends' jesting was partly true. They did spend most of their time together at church. **Where do you think Jeff and Susan had their minds set?**

Our culture seems to give teenagers the message that dating should be about seeking pleasure for yourself. Where do you think this message comes from?

The sinful nature is all about ME. What makes ME feel good? What is fun for ME? What will be best for ME in my future? We can focus our thoughts on ourselves and feed our sinful nature, or we can focus our thoughts on God and allow the Holy Spirit to lead our lives. The key to avoiding impurity is allowing the Spirit (instead of your sinful nature) to control your life.

So, dear brothers and sisters, you have no obligation whatsoever to do what your sinful nature urges you to do. For if you keep on following it, you will perish. But if through the power of the Holy Spirit you turn from it and its evil deeds, you will live. For all who are led by the Spirit of God are children of God (Rom. 8:12-14).

What do children of God do?

They are l_____ by the S_________ of G______.

Children of God are characterized by living according to the power of God. We don't avoid impurity by our own power. We avoid impurity by the power of the Holy Spirit.

FOUR: THE POWER OF THE SPIRIT

I have been crucified with Christ. I myself no longer live, but Christ lives in me. So I live my life in this earthly body by trusting in the Son of God, who loved me and gave himself for me (Gal. 2:19-20).

According to Paul, what was different about his life since he had become a Christian?

In his testimony, Juan told his congregation, "I am tired of doing things my way. From now on I am going to live my life according to God's rules."

The testimony sounded good, but what was wrong with it? Check two or more.

- ☐ **Juan would never be successful in keeping all of God's rules.**
- ☐ **Juan was still focused on his own abilities.**
- ☐ **Juan needed to allow Christ to live through him instead of trying to live for God.**

You may have heard people share well-meaning testimonies like Juan's. You may have even shared a testimony like that yourself. Hopefully by now you are thinking differently. You should have checked all of the above statements because all of them are problems.

POINT TO PONDER

Living a pure life is something I can't do on my own. I can only be successful at living a pure life by setting myself aside and allowing Christ to live in me.

This all sounds good, but how does a person allow Christ to live through him or her?

Here are a few hints:

1. Stay in the W_____ of G____.

How can a young person stay pure? By obeying your word and following its rules. I have tried my best to find you—don't let me wander from your commands. I have hidden your word in my heart, that I might not sin against you (Ps. 119:9-11).

You cannot follow God's commands on your own. However, spending time searching God's Word will help you to keep your mind focused on Him. It will help you to sense the leadership of the Spirit. God will use His Word to speak to you and help you to grow in your obedience to Him.

2. T______ a_______ from any s____ that God reveals to you as soon as you are aware of it.

If we say we have no sin, we are only fooling ourselves and refusing to accept the truth. But if we confess our sins to him, he is faithful and just to forgive us and to cleanse us from every wrong (1 John 1:8-9).

God never intended for us to allow sin in our lives. As soon as we realize that we have sinned against God, we should go to Him to ask for His forgiveness and His strength in turning away from our sin.

Sam had studied hard for the test, but he just couldn't figure out the answer to number 18. Sandra glanced at Sam's paper and noticed that he was struggling with the answer. She moved her paper for Sam to see her answer, so he copied it onto his test. He rationalized, "I was leaning toward that answer anyway." But the truth is, Sam knew he had cheated and he felt bad about it. Still, he got a perfect score on the test and received praise from his parents and his teacher. When the next test came up, he hadn't studied as much. Sandra gave him several answers on that test. He felt a little guilty, but it wasn't as bad as the first time. On the next test, he got most of his answers from Sandra and was able to give her a couple as well. He really didn't feel bad anymore. Cheating just seemed like a way for he and Sandra to help each other through the class.

That is the way sin works. The first time the Holy Spirit prods about a sin, it hurts. You realize that you are guilty of sin. The Spirit urges you to go to God for forgiveness, repent of what you did wrong, and seek to do anything you can to make it right. Ignore the Holy Spirit's prodding and you won't notice it quite as much the next time. It will become easier and easier to commit the sin.

If Sam had followed the Spirit's prodding, how would he have handled the situation?

It might have been painful for Sam to do the right thing after he had cheated. He needed to come clean about the cheating. He would have to give up the perfect score, which he hadn't earned. He would have to humble himself to admit his sin. It would have been hard for him to do.

If Sam had dealt with his sin in that way the first time, do you think he would have cheated the next time? Probably not. The sin would have been harder to commit the next time. When we handle sin God's way, we grow. Doing the right thing becomes easier. On the other hand, if we don't admit our sin, don't turn from it, don't try to make it right, it just gets easier. It seems to get harder to even hear the voice of the Holy Spirit speaking to us. Check out what Paul said:

Do not stifle the Holy Spirit (1 Thess. 5:19).

How would you put that verse in your own words?

When you deal with sin quickly, you are allowing Christ to live in you. When you stifle the Holy Spirit, you are pushing Christ aside and trying to live your own life.

3. Be a________________ to other b____________.

Two people can accomplish more than twice as much as one; they get a better return for their labor. If one person falls, the other can reach out and help. But people who are alone when they fall are in real trouble. And on a cold night, two under the same blanket can gain warmth from each other. But how can one be warm alone? A person standing alone can be attacked and defeated, but two can stand back-to-back and conquer. Three are even better, for a triple-braided cord is not easily broken (Eccl. 4:9-12).

What are some ways two or three Christians can help each other to walk with God?

The truth is that Christians were never supposed to be living their faith alone. When Barnabas was sent to help build up the new church in Antioch, what was the first thing he did? (See Acts 11:22-26.)

When Paul and Barnabas parted company and Paul set out on his own missionary journey without Barnabas, did he go alone? (See Acts 15:36-41.)

When Jesus sent out His disciples, did He send them out alone? (See Luke 10:1.)

God always has intended for us to depend on each other. Satan likes nothing better than to get a believer alone without the support of other Christians. **Describe a time that you committed a sin that you would not have committed if you had been hanging out with a Christian friend or your youth minister.**

If you want to stay close to Christ, stay close to other people who also want to stay close to Christ.

FIVE: TRUE LOVE WAITS

In session one, we studied God's expectation for us—a pure life. Purity certainly includes not having sex until you are married, but purity means a lot more than that. God expects us to be totally offered to Him, to be holy and honorable.

There is a problem. In our own power, we can't do it. We were all born with a sin nature. No matter how hard we try, we find ourselves committing sin because of the sin nature we carry around with us.

Fortunately, there is an answer. The answer is Jesus Christ. When we give our lives to Him, He makes us completely clean. He doesn't just help us to be a little better, He makes us completely pure again.

The Holy Spirit gives us the power to live purely. On our own, we do impure things. When we offer our lives to Christ and let Him live through us, we do what is right and pure. Letting Christ live through us can be a challenge, because it means denying ourselves. However, if we will stay in His Word, deal with sin as it arises in our lives, stay close to other people who want to allow Christ to live through them, and ask Christ for His help, He will live through us.

Closing Prayer: *Jesus, I can't live this pure life on my own. You can live a pure life through me. You are in me. Teach me to allow You to live Your pure life through me. Amen.*

Session 3

SECRET SIN

ONE: THERE IS NO SECRET SIN

Seth is a "computer geek." He loves spending time on the computer playing games, chatting with people from all over the world, and digging up the latest info on computer technology. He uses his skills at church by running the computer projections of the hymn lyrics. He even does some work on the youth ministry's Web site. His parents encourage his interest in computers and have helped him get the hardware he wanted for his bedroom. What his parents don't know is that many times late at night, Seth wanders onto the darker side of the Internet. One time he found some hard-core pornography Web sites; he now visits them regularly. At first he was just curious, but lately Seth has become obsessed with the vulgar images. He is glad his parents don't know how to track the Internet sites he visits.

We have a tendency to think that there are some sins we can keep hidden. Usually, these sins are the ones we commit in private. However, our secret sins may not be as private as we like to think. There are three reasons why no sin is truly secret.

FIRST: God sees our secret place.

Katrina sets some limits on her physical relationship with her boyfriend, but she knows that her standards are not as high as God's standards. She compromises because she is afraid her boyfriend will lose interest if she won't let him touch her in ways she knows are too sexual. After every date, she bounces past her parents with a smile. But when she goes to her room and looks in the mirror, she can sense God's Spirit telling her that her relationship with her boyfriend is wrong. No one else knows … but God knows.

"Am I a God who is only in one place?" asks the Lord. "Do they think I cannot see what they are doing? Can anyone hide from me? Am I not everywhere in all the heavens and earth?" asks the Lord (Jer. 23:23-24).

What does God say about the possibility of hiding anything from Him?

When you are all alone in your room, God is there. Whatever you do, whatever you look at, whatever you think about—God sees. In fact, if you are a Christian, He is not only with you; He is inside of you.

SECOND: Others probably know something is up.
Mary tapped on her mother's bedroom door. Her face was sullen as she came in and sat next to her mother on the bed. "I need to tell you something," Mary said.

"I was wondering when you were going to get around to telling me. You must have done something that is really eating you up," her mother responded.

Mary was a little surprised. "You already know what I'm going to tell you?" she asked.

Mary's mother stroked Mary's hair gently. "I don't know what you did, but I have been pretty sure for a couple of days that you were feeling guilty about something. What's up?"

Your parents may not be as perceptive as Mary's mother was. Your youth minister may be completely fooled by you. But most of the time you are trying to hide something, the people who know you best realize that something is wrong. They may not know what the problem is, but they can see that something is different.

Have you ever had a friend who was struggling with something he didn't want to tell you? How did you realize something was wrong? Describe the experience below.

The Lord looked with favor on Abel and his offering, but on Cain and his offering he did not look with favor. So Cain was very angry, and his face was downcast. Then the Lord said to Cain, "Why are you angry? Why is your face downcast?" (Gen. 4:4-6, NIV)

When Cain was angry, what did his face do?

God knows everything, but all He had to do was look at Cain's face to know something was up. The way people know something is up is that your face gives you away.

A glad heart makes a happy face;
a broken heart crushes the spirit (Prov. 15:13).

THIRD: Eventually it will all be known.

For everything that is hidden or secret will eventually be brought to light and made plain to all (Luke 8:17).

What does this verse say about secret sins?

Even if you can fool a lie detector test, even if you can "put on a happy face," one day it will all come out. In the end, there are no secret sins. Some secrets may not be known until the judgment day. But there is no doubt that anything done in secret will be exposed.

If you are involved in a secret sin right now, God knows about your sin. More than likely, others can see that something is not right. Eventually, everyone is going to know what you are doing. We only fool ourselves when we think there is such a thing as secret sin.

TWO: THERE IS NO HARMLESS SIN

Tad kept a soft-porn magazine under his mattress. He would only look through it occasionally. He reasoned that it didn't hurt anything. No one knew he had it, so it couldn't damage his witness, he thought. He figured that when he finally gets married, he won't need it anymore.

Did Tad's secret sin hurt anyone?

God says there are three very significant things that happen with every sin … even the sins that seem to harm no one.

Sin damages our fellowship with God.
Picture this: You went to the movies with your best friend. For some unknown reason, she tells your parents that she didn't go out with you that night and has no idea where you were. Your parents nail you with questions. They take away every privilege you have because they think you are lying to them. Worst of all, they tell you they can no longer trust you. You can't believe the lie your best friend told them.

Next time you see your friend, you'll give her a big hug and tell her how glad you are to be her friend. Right? No? Of course not! She hurt you. You will be focused on one thing: the lie she told.

The Bible says that all sin is committed against God. (See Ps. 51:4.) When you sin, you are doing something painful to God. When you start praying to Him as if nothing happened, can you see why God would be focused on your sin and not on the things you want to talk to Him about? However, God is not human. He will not cast us aside like a friend might. He understands what it is to be tempted. But there is still a sense in which our fellowship with Him is broken.

If I had not confessed the sin in my heart, my Lord would not have listened (Ps. 66:18).

When you have tried to hide sin from God, how did it affect your prayer life?

When we hang onto sin, then our fellowship with God is hurt.

Sin destroys us.

Because of your anger, my whole body is sick; my health is broken because of my sins. My guilt overwhelms me—it is a burden too heavy to bear. My wounds fester and stink because of my foolish sins. I am bent over and racked with pain. My days are filled with grief. A raging fever burns within me, and my health is broken. I am exhausted and completely crushed. My groans come from an anguished heart. You know what I long for, Lord; you hear my every sigh. My heart beats wildly, my strength fails, and I am going blind (Ps. 38:3-10).

David wrote this psalm after he realized that he had sinned against God. What did David say was happening to him as a result of his sins? Check two or more.

- ☐ **He was losing his health.**
- ☐ **He was enjoying life.**
- ☐ **His bones were weak.**
- ☐ **His wounds would not heal properly.**
- ☐ **He had a lot of friends.**
- ☐ **His back was in pain.**
- ☐ **He was weak.**
- ☐ **He had a bad heart.**

David sounds like a man in terrible pain. When we have secret, hidden sins, we are slowly killing ourselves. If you allow secret sin to hide in the dark corners of your life for very long it will destroy you.

Sin harms our future relationships.

Randy grew up in a Christian home and had become a Christian as a child. When he was a teenager, however, Randy started looking at pornography. In his college years, he moved from looking at pictures to visiting bars featuring nude dancers. When he married, he gave all that up. However, after a few years of marriage, Randy started looking at the same magazines behind his wife's back. She felt completely betrayed when she found one of Randy's "secret sins" hidden in the closet. When she saw him leaving a bar known for its nude dancers, she packed her bags and left with their two sons. Randy thought he could keep his secret sin in check, but the allure of the sin pattern he established in high school destroyed his marriage and his family.

Here is what can happen: You become involved in looking at pornography, calling phone-sex lines, or committing any other secret sexual sin. Eventually, it becomes a habit. You tell yourself that once you are married, you won't "need" this anymore. You stop for a while when you marry. One day you are thinking about what you used to do, and so you try it one more time. Bam! You're right back where you started. Only this time, it not only is destroying you; it is also destroying your family.

Throw off your old evil nature and your former way of life, which is rotten through and through, full of lust and deception. Instead, there must be a spiritual renewal of your thoughts and attitudes (Eph. 4:22-23).

What are we, as Christians, to do? Check two or more.
☐ **Put off our old way of life.**
☐ **Be made new in our mind (by Him).**
☐ **Put on our new righteous and holy self.**
☐ **Be careful about lack of church attendance.**

God forgave all your sin—past, present, and future—when you received Christ. God can and will heal you from the scars of past sins, even secret sins. But the more you invest in secret sin, the more difficult God's restoration will be.

THREE: THE TRAP

Satan tells us two lies about sin. He tells us we can keep sins secret and then he tells us that some sins are harmless. When we believe these lies, he is able to trap us in the snare called pornography.

Pornography comes through many avenues. Television, movies, music videos, the Internet, magazines, books; even coarse jokes can be pornographic. Pornography is more than just nudity. It is any form of media which excites your sensual nature and entices you to think and act sinfully. In the process we choose to believe several lies.

LIE ONE: Pornography is not addictive.
"Alcohol is addictive. Cocaine is addictive. There is nothing in pornography that addicts you. You choose to look at it. You could choose not to. It's all under your control."

The truth is you don't control pornography; it controls you. Look at the biblical example of King David.

Late one afternoon David got out of bed after taking a nap and went for a stroll on the roof of the palace. As he looked out over the city, he noticed a woman of unusual beauty taking a bath (2 Sam. 11:2).

What mistakes did David make?

I think that what the Bible means was that David noticed her, then kept on noticing her. Why do you think David was unable to stop at looking?

Look at what happened next:

He sent someone to find out who she was, and he was told, "She is Bathsheba, the daughter of Eliam and the wife of Uriah the Hittite." Then David sent for her; and when she came to the palace, he slept with her (2 Sam. 11:3-4).

What should have made David stop any attempt to see Bathsheba?

Why was David unable to stop when he knew this was wrong?

What resulted from David's looking?

You know the story. Eventually David's little secret led to murder. The allure of looking appeals to our sensual nature. It is very powerful. It grabs the heart of the person who begins looking and will not easily let go. It is very addictive.

LIE TWO: Pornography is not sinful.
There is a belief that just looking at pornography is not sinful. In fact, some even say they are "just admiring God's creation." Even in Jesus' day this lie persisted. But look what Jesus said about just looking.

"'You have heard that the law of Moses says, 'Do not commit adultery.' But I say, anyone who even looks at a woman with lust in his eye has already committed adultery with her in his heart'" (Matt. 5:27-28).

What was His conclusion about looking? Check one.
- ☐ **Look, but don't touch.**
- ☐ **If you look with lust you have committed adultery in your heart.**
- ☐ **The heart is tough to judge.**
- ☐ **The main sin is action, not looking.**

Looking with lust is just as sinful as any sexual sin. The whole point of pornography is to make people fantasize, to make people lust. Looking at pornography equals lust, equals sin.

LIE THREE: Pornography is not degrading.
One of the saddest things about pornography is what it does to people. Pornography takes something God created as good—the human body—and turns it into an object to be lusted after and fantasized about.

When they refused to acknowledge God, he abandoned them to their evil minds and let them do things that should never be done (Rom. 1:28).

When a person poses for a pornographic picture, she uses God's creation for sordid purposes. She loses the dignity that God gave her. When someone exposes people for money, he fails to respect God's precious creations. And when people view pornography, they are taking what God made and pronounced "very good" and making it base and dirty. People who participate in pornography are degrading God's creation and are doing "things that should never be done."

LIE FOUR: Pornography is not the problem.
In some ways, there is a bit of truth in this statement. The problem with using pornography goes deeper than just looking at "dirty" pictures. However, pornography is a large part of the problem.

"Your eye is a lamp for your body. A pure eye lets sunshine into your soul. But an evil eye shuts out the light and plunges you into darkness. If the light you think you have is really darkness, how deep that darkness will be" (Matt. 6:22-23).

What does this passage say about your eyes?

What enters your eyes can bring light or darkness to your soul. Pornography darkens the soul. When pornography is replaced by the light of Christ, the whole soul is lightened. Yes, there may be serious issues that lead a person to use pornography, but removing the pornography is the first step in dealing with those issues.

FOUR: ESCAPE

The chances are good that some who are studying this book have been dabbling with pornography. You may be deeply involved in pornography even though no one else knows. I hope you have gotten a clear picture of the truth of this secret sin. You may be asking, how do I deal with past (or present) failures when it comes to pornography?

The good news is that God wants to help you escape. It may not be easy. Some of you may have developed an addiction to these images that will be hard to break. But God will provide a way out.

But remember that the temptations that come into your life are no different from what others experience. And God is faithful. He will keep the temptation from becoming so strong that you can't stand up against it. When you are tempted, he will show you a way out so that you will not give in to it (1 Cor. 10:13).

What does this verse say about God's provision for escape?

POINT TO PONDER

No matter how big the secret sin in your life is, Christ in you is more powerful.

Here are some steps that usually are part of God's provision for your escape from a gripping sin. You may need more help. Don't hesitate to seek the counsel of a wise pastor or a Christian counselor.

STEP ONE: Know the truth.

"And you will know the truth, and the truth will set you free" (John 8:32).

We have done our best to present the truth about pornography in this chapter. Review this truth over and over again. Satan's best trick is to cause you to doubt the things you have learned. Hang onto the truth of God!

STEP TWO: Surrender to God.

In war when someone surrenders, they are saying "you win." In a spiritual war, you surrender to God. That means saying, "I can't beat pornography, but You can."

Oh, what a miserable person I am! Who will free me from this life that is dominated by sin? Thank God! The answer is in Jesus Christ our Lord (Rom. 7:24-25).

What is the only answer for being delivered from sinful self?

J________.

The answer is not a book or a strategy. The answer is a Person. When you surrender to Jesus, you stop trying to overcome sin on your own, and trust Him to work in your heart.

STEP THREE: Experience renewal.

Have you ever checked out a library book and then discovered that you needed it for more time? (I know some of you have never even been to the library, but work with me here.) When you need extra time, you renew it. You get a fresh start with the book. We need to learn how to get a fresh start with God everyday.

It may happen that you have a lustful thought or begin to desire to get involved in your secret sin sometime during the day. You realize you are not surrendered to Jesus anymore. At that point, stop and by faith pray something like, "Jesus, I believe You are in me. But it appears I, not You, am presently controlling my life. So, by faith, I turn it back over to You. I can't control my lust, but You can. Control my mind, my emotions, and my will right now."

STEP FOUR: Prepare for war.

You are in a war. You belong to Jesus, but Satan has not given up his war for your heart and mind. Unless you learn to actively defend yourself, you will become a casualty of war. Defense starts with God's armor.

Use every piece of God's armor to resist the enemy in the time of evil, so that after the battle you will still be standing firm. Stand your ground, putting on the sturdy belt of truth and the body armor of God's righteousness. For shoes, put on the peace that comes from the Good News, so that you will be fully prepared. In every battle you will need faith as your shield to stop the fiery arrows aimed at you by Satan. Put on salvation as your helmet, and take the sword of the Spirit, which is the word of God. Pray at all times and on every occasion in the power of the Holy Spirit. Stay alert and be persistent in your prayers for all Christians everywhere (Eph. 6:13-18).

In the battle against the secret sin of pornography, there are three pieces of armor that are especially important.

The Helmet of Salvation - This is a battle of the mind. The helmet guards the mind. When our mind knows that we belong to Christ and that He is in us, we don't have to fall for the enemy's lies.

The Shield of Faith - By faith Jesus lives, not me. This was Paul's shield. See Galatians 2:20. By faith he allowed Jesus to do the fighting.

The Sword of the Spirit - This is the Word of God. When Jesus was tempted, He quoted Scripture. See Matthew 4:1–11. God's Word is an offensive weapon we can use in this battle.

STEP FIVE: Find a partner.
Christ supplies another valuable resource: other Christians.

Run from anything that stimulates youthful lust. Follow anything that makes you want to do right. Pursue faith and love and peace, and enjoy the companionship of those who call on the Lord with pure hearts (2 Tim. 2:22).

What did Paul tell Timothy to do? Check one.
- ☐ **Watch out for sin.**
- ☐ **Watch out for the youth.**
- ☐ **Flee evil desires.**
- ☐ **Flee evil desires with those who call upon the Lord.**

Find a person of the same sex that will serve as your accountability partner. This person must be someone you can trust, someone who is willing to ask you the hard questions about your secret sin, and someone who will pray with you.

Ask God to lead you through these steps. Remember that it is He who provides the way of escape, not us. It is He who works in us telling us the truth, allowing us to surrender, renewing our mind, fighting the war, and giving us an accountability partner.

On our own, we will fail. But God always leads us to victory!

FIVE: TRUE LOVE WAITS

God has called us to a life of purity. Our sin nature makes it impossible for us to do that on our own, but God gives us the power to live a pure life. He gives us His righteousness and leads us to righteous living.

Still, it is easy to believe that we can keep some sins secret. We may believe that we can hide sexual sins, like the use of pornography. But no sin will ultimately be secret and all sin will eventually destroy us. Pornography is a trap. It is all the more dangerous as we try to keep it secret. But the good news is that we don't have to live like that. We have Christ living inside of us. As He teaches us the truth, we start to be free. As we surrender, and as we admit we can't live purely on our own, He starts to do it through us. Then we allow him to renew our minds. Several times a day, we allow Him to renew our minds and make us newly surrendered.

Now we are ready for the fight. This battle isn't a one-time thing. It is going on everyday. So He brings another person to you—someone He will use to hold you accountable. If you desire to live a life of purity, pray the following prayer.

Closing Prayer: *Jesus, I know You are alive in me. Yet at times I have listened to the lies of Satan. Right now I acknowledge that I can't beat Satan or his traps. By faith, I now ask You to begin freeing me from the traps in my life. Teach me the truth in this area that I might totally rely upon You.*

Session 4

LIVING IN PURITY

ONE: TOO FAR?

Students filled the camp auditorium. They were excited about what was going to happen at this big winter retreat. The speaker was a pastor with a reputation of knowing students well. They were sure that God was going to speak to them.

As the speaker took the stage, he began sharing a message on sexual purity. The students knew that this would be one of the topics for the weekend. Many of them took out notebooks to make notes on the speaker's suggestions for avoiding sex before marriage. He shared his testimony of how he had been involved in immoral relationships as a lost teenager and how Christ had saved him and cleansed him from sin. He told how God had brought him to his wife, the most wonderful woman he had ever known. Then he offered advice on how to stay pure. "God has someone special for you. Until you find the person you will spend your life with, don't have a physical relationship at all. Hold hands if you like someone, but don't do anything beyond that. If you never move to kissing, chances are you will never move to anything more."

The students sat in silence. This was a more extreme view than they had ever heard before. Many of them were angry. "The Bible never says, 'don't kiss,'" they told their youth leaders. "How dare he tell us to be so backward?"

That preacher may have been extreme in his advice. Still, there was an element of truth in it. Most of us want to know where the line is. How far can we go before we are committing sin? That is true in many areas of life. We want to know how nice we have to be to someone to meet the Bible's standard of loving everyone. We want to know how much stuff we can have before we have sinned by becoming a lover of money. But it is true more of our sexual relationships than any other area of life. If holding hands is OK, then is kissing? If kissing is OK, then is heavy kissing? If heavy kissing is OK, then is petting? If that's OK, then what else is?

POINT TO PONDER

We like to ask, "How far is too far?" A better question for a believer is, "How can I best honor God?"

What difference would it make in your life and your relationships if you asked, "How can I best honor God?" instead of "How far is too far?"

Check out God's desire for your bodies.

Do not let any part of your body become a tool of wickedness, to be used for sinning. Instead, give yourselves completely to God since you have been given new life. And use your whole body as a tool to do what is right for the glory of God (Rom. 6:13).

God does set boundaries for us to live pure lives. The goal, however, should not be to see how close to the line you can get without crossing over it. The goal should be to try to do everything you can to honor God with your body.

So, where are the boundaries?

TWO: PHYSICAL BOUNDARIES

To understand the physical boundaries, you have to understand the true purpose for physical love between a man and a woman.

This explains why a man leaves his father and mother and is joined to his wife, and the two are united into one (Gen. 2:24).

According to this verse, what is the reason for sexual love? Check one.

- ☐ **For pure fun**
- ☐ **To unite two into one**
- ☐ **For procreation**
- ☐ **To prevent boredom**

God designed physical, sexual love to knit two lives together. The physical pleasure was designed to bring a husband and wife into a bond where they become one, a bond that nothing can break. God created this physical love with that one goal in mind, to bind a man and a woman together for life.

God created us to desire that one-flesh relationship. When we begin a physical relationship with someone of the opposite sex, it is supposed to lead to sexual intercourse. Because of the way God made us, heavy kissing, petting, and making out leads to intercourse. That is the way it is supposed to work in marriage.

In biblical times, people found their marriage partner much differently than they do today. There wasn't a long period of dating. People went from seeing each other clothed head-to-toe to being married. Most people in that time knew very little physically about the person they married. Consequently, there is little written in the Bible about how dangerous things like heavy kissing can be between people who think they are in love.

When unmarried Christians start getting physical with each other, their body reacts no differently than the married person's. His or her body wants to have intercourse because it is the way it is made.

What is God's standard? Here is the way Paul said it:

God wants you to be holy, so you should keep clear of all sexual sin (1 Thess. 4:3).

What does all of this mean practically? When you begin a physical relationship, the body begins to want more. The mind has raced ahead, and it is ultimately going to one place—sex. That's the way we are made. Now, the couple might fight off the desire and stop. But they have tested the limit. Are they keeping clear of sexual sin? Not really. They are testing the limit.

Where is the limit? Ask yourself, can you kiss a boyfriend or girlfriend without wanting to do more? Can you hug each other without wanting to do more? For some couples, brief kissing will be fine. For many couples, anything more than holding hands will be too much. Unless you are dead, the heavy, make-out type of kissing is across the boundary because it makes your body want to go to the next level. You may not go there, but your body desires to.

Girls, be careful here. It may be fine for you to have your boyfriend hold you for a long time. However, your boyfriend's body may be screaming to move on toward sex. If both of you are going to honor Christ with your bodies, you will need to be careful not to step over the line for the other.

Think about it. What is the limit you can go to without your body wanting more? Do you need to make any changes in a physical relationship you are in?

THREE: EMOTIONAL BOUNDARIES

It may sound strange to you, but physical boundaries in your relationships are not the only boundaries you should watch out for. Equally as dangerous as crossing the physical boundaries, is crossing the emotional boundaries God desires for your heart.

The problem often begins as we give our heart away to someone other than God. Someone says hello to us twice in the same day and offers us a seat in the lunchroom, and we are "in love."

Whom have I in heaven but you?
I desire you more than anything on earth (Ps. 73:25).

In a pop song, the words of this psalm might be written from a man to a woman he loved. But they aren't. This is how the psalmist described his love for God. It is the kind of love relationship that God desires with you. God desires to be your everything: your best friend, your lover, your constant companion.

There are two ways that people can "fall in love." One is that they take the passionate love they should have for God, and give it to each other instead. The other is that they passionately love God, and He draws them together; out of their mutual love for Him, a passionate love for each other grows.

Which description of "falling in love" honors God?

As we commit everything to Him in prayer, an awesome thing happens.

Don't worry about anything; instead, pray about everything. Tell God what you need, and thank him for all he has done. If you do this, you will experience God's peace, which is far more wonderful than the human mind can understand. His peace will guard your hearts and minds as you live in Christ Jesus (Phil. 4:6-7).

Who is in charge of guarding our hearts?

As you are allowing God to guard your heart, practice the following behavior by faith with someone you date. Realize that some emotional things should be left for marriage.

- Don't say, "I love you," when what you mean is, "I think you are pretty, nice, or fun to be with."
- Avoid telling everything about yourself to the person you date.
- Have many friends, not just the person you date.
- Be careful about the way you spend your time together. Enjoy the time, but plan to do more than just stare in each other's eyes.
- Don't talk about, "if we were married..."

The key to staying within physical and emotional boundaries is to allow God to apply them to your heart. How willing are you to allow God to place these physical and emotional boundaries on your heart?

Since you have been raised to new life with Christ, set your sights on the realities of heaven, where Christ sits at God's right hand in the place of honor and power (Col. 3:1).

FOUR: SETTING STANDARDS

Carl was a senior in high school when he found Christ. His dating relationships had been pretty lousy before that. He knew that as a Christian, his standards for dating would have to change. He decided to talk it over with his Sunday School teacher, Dan.

The next Sunday before church, Dan and Carl met at a little coffee house. Carl talked about a lot of the mistakes he had made in dating before he became a Christian. "I used to just look for girls who were really good-looking. Now, I know I need better standards. I've written down my dating standards and I wanted to see what you thought." Dan nodded and Carl began reading through his list. He wanted a girl with brains *and* looks. He wanted someone who would at least come to church with him. He wanted someone who was willing to take the physical relationship slowly.

Carl looked up. "Well, what do you think? Am I getting all the standards that I should have as a Christian?" Carl asked.

Dan frowned. "I think there are some problems with the standards you've come up with," he told Carl.

What do you think? Was Carl on the right track? Do you see any problem with Carl setting those standards for dating?

Here's the big problem. The standards were Carl's. Who should be setting the standards for a Christian's dating life?

How can a young person stay pure? By obeying your word and following its rules (Ps. 119:9).

What does Psalm 119:9 tell us about living a pure life? Check one.

- ☐ **God uses His Word to bring a standard of purity.**
- ☐ **Look for purity in the words of your leaders.**
- ☐ **Purity changes over the years.**
- ☐ **It is tough to be pure.**

God has a standard for dating; it is found in the Bible. American dating is not in the Bible. However, God's standards about how people of opposite sexes are to relate to each other hold true in ancient Israel, modern America, or anywhere else. Let's look at some standards He has set.

STANDARD ONE: Date Jesus before you date others.
This may sound strange, but Jesus desires to be our first love. Look at the message of Jesus to the church at Ephesus:

> You have patiently suffered for me without quitting. But I have this complaint against you. You don't love me or each other as you did at first! Look how far you have fallen from your first love! Turn back to me again (Rev. 2:3-5).

You may really want a boyfriend or girlfriend. There is nothing wrong with that. But don't chase the boys or girls all over the school. Instead, focus your heart and your desire on truly loving the Lord. Love Him first; trust God for the rest.

STANDARD TWO: Date only strong, growing Christians.
The most important thing in Drew's life is Jesus. Maggie wants to date Drew. Maggie is pretty, funny, and sweet. However, the most important thing in Maggie's life is having fun. Maggie and Drew are moving in two

different directions. Drew may very well have some influence on Maggie, but it is almost certain that Maggie will also pull Drew a little off course. Surely Maggie cannot help Drew grow closer to Christ while she is pulling away from Him. That's what this verse is all about:

Don't team up with those who are unbelievers. How can goodness be a partner with wickedness? How can light live with darkness? (2 Cor. 6:14)

As you grow in Christ, you will long to be in a dating relationship with someone who also allows Christ to live through her or him. Look for these specific things in someone you consider dating. Even more, seek to make these things true for yourself.

1. Jesus is his or her life, not just a part of his or her life. (See Deut. 6:5.)
2. He or she has a humble and sensitive heart. (See Ps. 51:17.)
3. He or she is focused first on Christ and then on the needs of others—not focused on you! (See 2 Cor. 5:20.)
4. He or she is grounded in God's Word. The two of you agree on the basics of the faith. (See 1 Tim. 6:3-4.)
5. He or she has a strong and consistent time alone with God. His or her time with God takes priority over time with you. (See Ps. 84:10.)

STANDARD THREE: Allow God to bring the one you date. Many times even strong Christians go out and try to find a person to date and even marry. God wants you to trust Him in every area of your life, especially in the area of dating (or not dating).

Take delight in the Lord, and he will give you your heart's desires (Ps. 37:4).

What are we instructed to do? Check one.

☐ Find the desire of our heart.
☐ Delight ourselves in God.
☐ Seek help from friends.
☐ Develop a list of people to date.

What does God promise to do? Check one.

☐ Keep all our thoughts to Himself.
☐ Give us the desire of our heart.
☐ Take our desires into counsel.
☐ Finish the work of creation.

Our role is to delight ourselves in Him. When that happens, our heart becomes His heart. In a way, it isn't even our heart anymore; it is all Him. When that happens, He gives us the desires of our heart. After all, it is His heart now—His desires. When you try to find who you want to date, you may be getting ahead of God. When you trust Him to bring you the desire of your heart, He will do it. He will bring that person in His time, not your time.

Are you willing to allow Him to bring the person you date to you? Check one.

☐ Yes
☐ No
☐ I don't know

STANDARD FOUR: Never compromise.

Danny met Teresa at church camp and figured she must be a growing Christian. Teresa invited Danny on a walk, then asked if she could kiss him. What would any red-blooded, American boy say? It went farther than a kiss. Danny actually enjoyed it. He'd never had a girl be so aggressive with him. A few weeks after camp, Teresa invited him to spend a weekend with her and her parents. Since Teresa's parents would be there the whole time, Danny's parents allowed him to go.

However, Danny had a pretty good idea that Teresa had more in mind than hanging out with her folks. He thought he could go and just say no if things got too heavy. Warning! Danger! Danger!

It is so easy for us to compromise and give in a little because of the way we feel, even when we want our lives to be truly pure.

So don't get tired of doing what is good. Don't get discouraged and give up, for we will reap a harvest of blessing at the appropriate time (Gal. 6:9).

How would you put Paul's words to the Galatians in your own words?

When you get home from camp you are so high on Jesus that you are going to be a completely different person. You are obedient to your parents. You get up early every morning to have your time alone with God. You avoid going to places where you know you will be tempted to use foul language, or drink, or make fun of other people. You do all of that for how long? A week? Three days? What happens? You get tired of doing good. How can Christians get tired of doing good? Remember Session 2? We have a sin nature that constantly pulls at us.

How do you "never compromise"? Check one.
☐ **Lock yourself in a closet.**
☐ **Walk around wearing a blindfold.**
☐ **Take lots of cold showers.**
☐ **Walk in the Spirit.**

It may sound pretty cryptic, but the answer is to consistently walk in God's Spirit. Check out what Paul said:

So I advise you to live according to your new life in the Holy Spirit. Then you won't be doing what your sinful nature craves (Gal. 5:16).

That sounds good, but how do you do it? I'm glad you asked.

1. Spend time with God consistently.

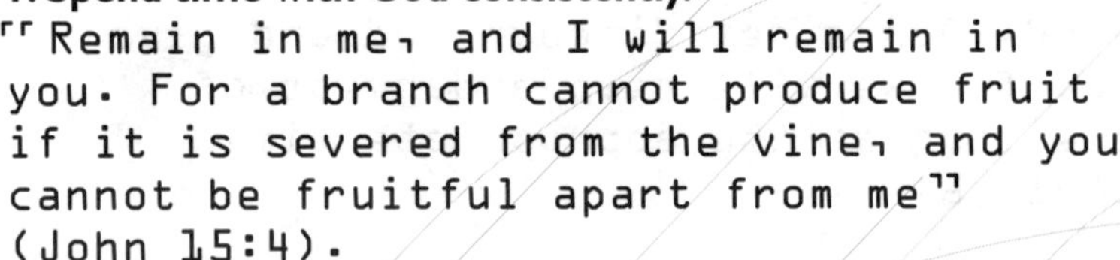

"Remain in me, and I will remain in you. For a branch cannot produce fruit if it is severed from the vine, and you cannot be fruitful apart from me" (John 15:4).

If you are not meeting God daily, you have already decided to fail. Sure, you can miss a day or two and still keep close to God. But if you don't have a habit of spending time with God, you will not have His power for living. You will not be walking in His Spirit.

2. Be faithful in the little things.

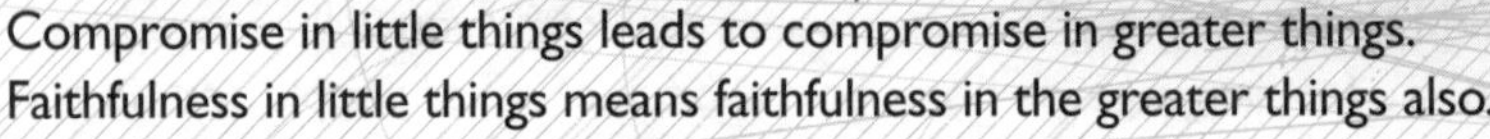

Compromise in little things leads to compromise in greater things. Faithfulness in little things means faithfulness in the greater things also.

"Unless you are faithful in small matters, you won't be faithful in large ones. If you cheat even a little, you won't be honest with greater responsibilities" (Luke 16:10).

Guys, do you lust over pictures in the swimsuit edition of a magazine? Girls, do your thoughts about the latest pop star honor God? These may be little things, but win the battle there and you will be ready for bigger battles. Trust the conviction of the Spirit in little things and you will know that you are walking with Him when tougher issues come.

3. Turn to God when you fail.

Hannah got caught up in the jokes at a party. She was a Christian, as were many of the people there. Nevertheless, one dirty joke led to another. She found herself laughing out loud at jokes that she knew in her heart were ungodly. When she got home, she thought, "I've ruined my witness to my non-Christians friends. How could God ever forgive me? It would be better if I wasn't a Christian; at least then I wouldn't be putting God in a negative light when I do something like that."

When we fail, the enemy will always try to tell us that God can never forgive us. Satan makes us feel that even if God did, we could never forgive ourselves for dragging His name through the mud. The truth is that God knows we will fail. When you do, run to His open arms for forgiveness. He loves you. He will reinstate you. He will show you how to make your sin right to the extent that you can.

My dear children, I am writing this to you so that you will not sin. But if you do sin, there is someone to plead for you before the Father. He is Jesus Christ, the one who pleases God completely (1 John 2:1).

4. Never quit.

Have you ever heard of Demas? Read how Paul described him:

Demas has deserted me because he loves the things of this life and has gone to Thessalonica (2 Tim. 4:10).

We don't know if Demas ever returned to the faith. The Bible says nothing more about him after this verse. For the rest of history, Demas was known as an obscure Christian who gave up. He abandoned the work of the Lord because he loved the world too much.

I don't know about you, but that is not the way I want to be remembered. Paul failed. So did Peter. What was the difference in those men and Demas?

They didn't quit. They received the forgiveness of Christ and started again. They continued to walk in the Spirit, even after they had failed.

FIVE: TRUE LOVE WAITS

God has called you to a life of purity. If you are really going to live the life that God has called you to, the wrong question is, "How far is too far?" The idea is not to see how close to sin you can get. The right question is, "How can I best honor God with my life?"

God has given us boundaries, both in terms of our physical and emotional relationships. The boundary of our physical relationship is to not go far enough that we find our body wanting more. The boundary of our emotional relationship is to focus on God first.

There are godly standards for the Christian in dating. They have nothing to do with what your date looks like. They have everything to do with your commitment to Christ. You should date Jesus first, date only growing Christians, allow God to bring your dating partners, and never compromise.

If you are ready to make God's standards yours, pray this prayer.

Closing Prayer: *Dear Lord, I desire for You to live through me in sexual purity. Apply Your standards and Your boundaries to my life. I give You permission to write these things on my heart; not that I would be legalistic or rigid, but rather that I would live this part of my life by faith, You living in me.*

Session 5

MAKING A COMMITMENT TO PURITY

ONE: IT'S A MARATHON

"So, do you want to run the marathon with me?" Jordan's dad asked. Jordan had never been much of a runner, but he was a good athlete. He had been thinking it might be fun to run a marathon with his dad. When he had mentioned it, his dad seemed really pleased. "What do you think?" his dad asked him.

"I guess I can try," Jordan told his dad. His dad frowned. "What?" Jordan asked.

"I'm not sure you understand, Jordan," his dad responded. "If we do this, we need to start training right now. We're going to have to get up early every morning, because you don't want to be training in the heat after school. We'll start slow, but we will be running 40 or 50 miles a week as we get closer to the race. I'd love to do this together, but I don't think you will do it unless you are really committed."

"Wow," was all Jordan said. He hated to even ask how early he would have to get up. His dad was right, of course. If he just decided day by day whether he felt like training, he never would feel like it. Still, he liked the idea of spending so much time with his dad. "Count me in," he told his dad. "I'm going to do it." His dad looked at him skeptically. "Seriously Dad, I'm going to do it—early morning training and all. And I'm going to enjoy finishing the race with you. It's going to be great!"

When you tell someone you ran a marathon, they ask, "Did you finish?" If you tell them you played a football game or a tennis match, they ask you, "Did you win?" But they don't ask you whether you won the marathon. (The winner was probably a 90-pound guy who has spent his whole life running with very few stops to eat or sleep.) Marathons are not about winning. They are about finishing. It's the same with True Love Waits. The goal is to finish, but the race will take you a lifetime.

If you approach a commitment to purity by saying, "I'm going to try to live a pure life," you are probably going to fail. When it is convenient to live purely, you will. When it gets tough, you will crumble. Those who live consistently pure lives have made a commitment to gut it out, no matter how tough it gets. They keep going regardless of how they feel.

TWO: A COMMITMENT BY FAITH

A True Love Waits commitment basically is a promise made to God, to your parents, to your friends, and even to your future spouse and future children. There are examples of significant promises like this in the Bible. The earliest one is a vow that Jacob made.

Then Jacob made this vow: "If God will be with me and protect me on this journey and give me food and clothing, and if he will bring me back safely to my father, then I will make the Lord my God. This memorial pillar will become a place for worshiping God, and I will give God a tenth of everything he gives me" (Gen. 28:20-22).

What does Jacob vow in this passage? Check two or more.

☐ **Not to have sex**
☐ **To give back to God a tenth, or tithe**
☐ **To build an altar to God**
☐ **To stop cussing**

It may seem like Jacob was trying to make a deal with God rather than make a vow. In truth, Jacob's vow was a response to a promise God had already made to him. God had appeared to Jacob in his sleep at the top of a stairway with angels going up and down it.

At the top of the stairway stood the Lord, and he said, "I am the Lord, the God of your grandfather Abraham and the God of your father, Isaac. The ground you are lying on belongs to you. I will give it to you and your descendants. Your descendants will be as numerous as the dust of the earth! They will cover the land from east to west and from north to south. All the families of the earth will be blessed through you and your descendants. What's more, I will be with you, and I will protect you wherever you go. I will someday bring you safely back to this land. I will be with you constantly until I have finished giving you everything I have promised" (Gen. 28:13-15).

God appeared to Jacob in a dream. What did God promise Jacob?

I will be w______ y_____.
I will p__________ y_____.
I will b________ y_____ s__________ b_______ to this land.
I will b____ w______ y_____ c____________.

When Jacob made his vow, it was like he was saying, "God if that really was you in my dream, then here is what I am going to do."

A vow, a commitment, or a pledge is really a response to what God has already done. It is a response to the grace of God.

Do you remember the story of Zacchaeus? Jesus was walking through Jericho and a short tax collector named Zacchaeus wanted to see him. So Zacchaeus climbed into a tree to see over the crowd. Jesus stopped and told him to come down because Jesus was going to eat with him. Jesus showed him love and compassion. Others shunned Zacchaeus because he was a tax collector, but Jesus went to his house for dinner. Do you remember the rest of the story?

Meanwhile, Zacchaeus stood there and said to the Lord, "I will give half my wealth to the poor, Lord, and if I have overcharged people on their taxes, I will give them back four times as much!"

Jesus responded, "Salvation has come to this home today, for this man has shown himself to be a son of Abraham. And I, the Son of Man, have come to seek and save those like him who are lost" (Luke 19:8-10).

What had Jesus done for Zacchaeus?

In response, what did Zacchaeus pledge to do?

What has God done in your life that would prompt you to commit to purity?

The problem with making vows and making commitments is that we often fail to keep our commitments. Consider marriage. Almost every marriage vow includes the words, "till death do us part." Yet about half of marriages end in divorce.

Many adults ask, "How can you ask students to make a commitment to sexual purity? What happens if they fail to keep the commitment?" These are good questions. You should never enter into a covenant commitment with God half-heartedly. It is serious business.

So, how do you keep your commitment to sexual purity? The truth is you can't … if you are trying to do it on your own. You will need God's power to remain sexually pure.

Trust in the Lord with all your heart; do not depend on your own understanding. Seek his will in all you do, and he will direct your paths (Prov. 3:5-6).

What are people encouraged to do? Check one.

☐ **Trust in God**
☐ **Trust not in themselves**
☐ **Be as good as they can be**
☐ **Find someone to trust**

People get in trouble when they make a commitment trusting in their own power to carry it out. That is why so many marriages fail—human effort is almost never enough. Instead, God wants us to trust in Him.

Habakkuk 2:4 is an Old Testament verse that is quoted three times in the New Testament. It says, "The righteous will live by their faith." The meaning is simple when it comes to making a commitment. A commitment to sexual purity is a promise to live purely, to live righteously. We cannot do that in our own power, but we can by faith. By faith, we trust that He living in us will not only make the commitment, but He in us will carry it out.

I am sure that God, who began the good work within you, will continue his work until it is finally finished on that day when Christ Jesus comes back again (Phil. 1:6).

Who will begin any commitment (good work) you might make?

Who will carry out any commitment (good work) you might make?

POINT TO PONDER

The key to a commitment to sexual purity is to make the commitment by faith in Jesus and trust Him to give you the power to keep the commitment.

THREE: CHARACTERISTICS OF A COMMITMENT

Which of these would you say are real commitments? Check two or more.

- ☐ **Jenna tells you that she will try to come over to your house after school to study.**
- ☐ **Tyrone gives Keeley his class ring. She asks what it means. He says, "You know."**
- ☐ **Jeffrey tells his mom he will take the trash out before school in the morning.**
- ☐ **Kim says that she hopes to be at your birthday party on Saturday, but she has a lot to do over the weekend.**
- ☐ **At camp Aaron feels convicted by God to have a daily quiet time. He tells his youth group that starting the morning after they get home, he is going to get up at least 10 minutes early every morning so he can spend time with God. "I won't eat," he tells them, "until I've spent at least a few minutes in God's Word." He asks the group to check on him and make sure he is doing it.**

What makes you know Aaron's commitment is real?

Have you ever heard anyone make the kind of "commitment" like Kim made? If she had been talking to me, I would have assumed that she wasn't coming. And yet, some people seem to make True Love Waits commitments in the same way. "Well, I'm under a lot of sexual pressure, but I'm going to sign a card and hope for the best." Right!

A real commitment takes more than that. True commitments, whether you're talking about sexual purity or about taking out the trash, have these things in common.

1. The commitment will be specific.
Look back at the promise Zacchaeus made (p. 69). What specific things did he pledge to do? Check two or more.
☐ Stop smoking
☐ Give half of his possessions to the poor
☐ Go to synagogue on Saturday
☐ Repay those he had cheated

Jesus was pleased with Zacchaeus' commitment; He even said salvation had come to Zacchaeus. Wow! Jesus wasn't saying that Zacchaeus was saved by his pledge; you can't be saved by your good works.

Why did Jesus say that Zacchaeus was saved after hearing his commitment?

If Zacchaeus had said, "Lord, from now on I'm going to be a better person," that would not have meant much. When the Holy Spirit deals with us, He is very specific. Jesus said that Zacchaeus had experienced salvation because he was making promises that came directly from the work of the Holy Spirit in his life, convicting him of specific sins. It is not always the case that specific commitments are from God. But commitments that are general in nature are an indication of human works.

See if you can distinguish between specific and general commitments. Check the commitments below that appear to be specific. Check two or more. (Note: You are not committing to these things. You are just determining which are specific.)

- ☐ **I will not have sex until marriage.**
- ☐ **I will try not to go too far on a date.**
- ☐ **I will not passionately kiss my date.**
- ☐ **I will date only nice people.**
- ☐ **I will pray before each date.**
- ☐ **I will not watch movies that seem too bad.**
- ☐ **I will not watch movies with any nudity.**
- ☐ **I will do my best to be pure.**

2. The commitment will be public.

There are a lot of "Secret Agent Christians" in the world today. Only God knows who they are! This is not God's way. God intends for your faith to be public and your commitment to Him to be public.

Danny was living a sexually pure life. He intended to save sex for marriage. But, in the locker room at Danny's school, that wasn't a popular commitment to have. So Danny occasionally made up stories about sleeping with girls. **How do you think the other guys in the locker room viewed Danny's commitment to Christ?**

"If a person is ashamed of me and my message, I, the Son of Man, will be ashamed of that person when I return in my glory and in the glory of the Father and the holy angels" (Luke 9:26).

What did Jesus say about those that are ashamed of Him and His words?

Telling people, especially other Christians, what God is calling you to do, does several things. As you share your commitment with others, God will solidify your commitment in your own life. God also will use you to challenge others to make commitments to Him. And God will use others who know of your commitment to hold you accountable for that commitment.

3. The commitment will be voluntary.

Sometimes when a group of youth are studying True Love Waits materials there is pressure from the group for everyone to make the commitment. Although positive peer pressure is better than negative peer pressure, a true commitment is not the result of pressure.

When you make a vow to the Lord your God, be prompt in doing whatever you promised him. For the Lord your God demands that you promptly fulfill all your vows. If you don't, you will be guilty of sin. However, it is not a sin to refrain from making a vow (Deut. 23:21-22).

What does this verse say about not making a vow?

If you r__________ from m__________ a v______, you will n____ be g________.

Failure to make a commitment is, in and of itself, not a sin! Sexual immorality is obviously a sin whether or not you make a commitment. God may be calling you to make a commitment to purity, but the choice is still yours. Choose carefully.

It is better to say nothing than to promise something that you don't follow through on (Eccl. 5:5).

FOUR: NAILING DOWN YOUR COMMITMENT

By this time in the study, God may have been working on your heart. In order to make a commitment to God, yourself, your family, your friends, your church, your future mate and children, and even the world, there are three things you need to do.

First: Identify the commitment.
When the rich, young ruler came to Jesus in Matthew 19:16-21, Jesus was more than willing to tell the young man what he had to do. But the key to getting Jesus to tell us what we must do is found in verse 16 of the story.

Someone came to Jesus with this question: "Teacher, what good things must I do to have eternal life?" (Matt. 19:16)

What did the man do when he came to Jesus? He a________.

Have you asked God what commitment He wants you to make? Pray something like this, "Jesus, I am willing to make the commitment You want me to in the area of purity. Show me the commitment You are bringing to my life."

When He shows you the commitment He wants you to make, write it in the space below.

Second: Privately affirm the commitment in your spirit.
Although Jesus lives in you, your spirit can still rebel against Him. Allow God to change your heart so that you desire purity for your own life.

Pray something like this, "Jesus, control my spirit. Create a total desire in my inward being for this commitment. Help me to trust You to live this commitment out through me."

Paul desired for this very thing for the people in Thessalonica.

Now may the God of peace make you holy in every way, and may your whole spirit and soul and body be kept blameless until that day when our Lord Jesus Christ comes again. God, who calls you, is faithful; he will do this (1 Thess. 5:23-24).

What was Paul desiring for them? Check two or more.
- ☐ **God to sanctify them**
- ☐ **God to keep them—body, soul, and spirit**
- ☐ **God to do the work**
- ☐ **The people to work harder at Christianity**

Third: Make your commitment public.
This is the final, but crucial, step. If God is in your commitment, you will want to make it public. In order to make it public, you can use the True Love Waits Commitment Card. The commitment God has called you to will be more specific than what is written on the card, but the card will be a good place to start. Your youth leader can provide a copy of the card for you, or you can find out how to get copies of the card by visiting the True Love Waits Web site at *www.truelovewaits.com*. You can sign the card and make the decision public in a worship service with your youth group or church.

FIVE: TRUE LOVE WAITS

Through this entire study, you have seen God's desire for you to be sexually pure. Hopefully, you have been challenged to live a life of purity. You have also seen that our own human efforts to live a pure life are doomed to failure. It is only by the power of God working in and through us that we are able to live in purity.

Perhaps God has been speaking to you about committing your life to sexual purity. If so, you will need to first listen to what God is telling you. He probably is speaking to you very specifically about how He wants you to live. You must affirm in your heart your desire to live a pure life, then let others know of your commitment. Trust God, and He will guide you to the life of purity that He desires for you.

As you close this study, pray the following prayer.

Closing Prayer: *Jesus, I thank You for how You are working wonderfully in me. I look forward to what You are going to do tomorrow in and through my life. I desire nothing less than to be totally given to You, to be pure. I thank You that You have made this possible and will continue to make it a reality.*

LEADER GUIDE

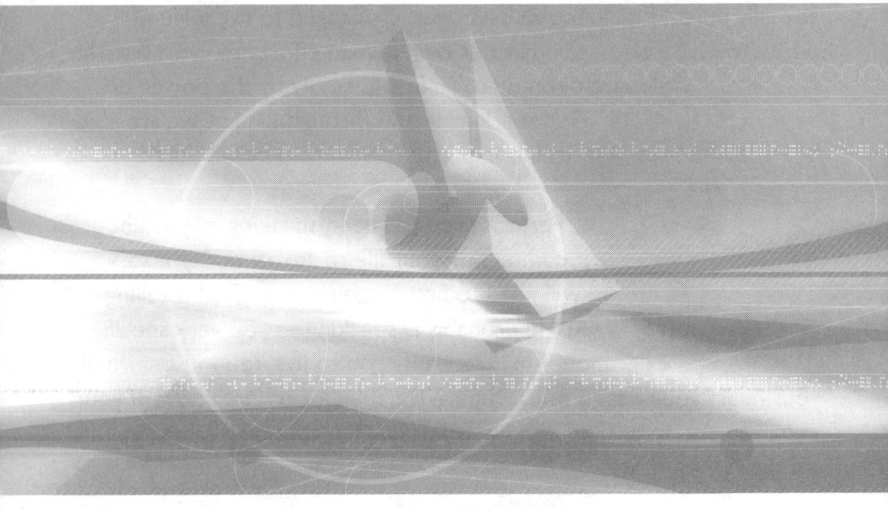

It is possible to lead your group in a study of *Living Pure Inside Out* without using this leader guide. But for a more effective route than just having students read the material and answer the questions, we recommend using these plans to involve students in the learning process. Even if you use this guide, every student will still need his or her own book.

This leader guide can be used in a large- or small-group setting to teach the five Bible studies in this book. The teaching steps correspond directly to the sections in each study. You may not desire to use every suggestion in each step. Feel free to use your own ideas to engage your group in active learning.

At the end of each session guide are the answers to the response activities from that session. (Answers to opinion or personal questions are not included.) There are also additional ideas for use with DiscipleNow or Youth Retreat settings.

Session 1

Overview: In this session students will discover what true purity is all about and find out where purity begins.

Before the session:

- ☐ Place a chalkboard or dry erase board in the room.
- ☐ Bring extra pens and Bibles.
- ☐ For step 1: Provide three-by-five inch cards, pens, and a copy of this book for each student.
- ☐ For step 2: Write the "Point to Ponder" (p. 9) on poster board. Provide large sheets of paper and markers.
- ☐ For step 3: Record a video from TV showing how messed up the world is. Be sure it is appropriate for a church setting.
- ☐ For step 4: Enlist a student to share his or her personal testimony.

STEP 1 As students arrive, give each a three-by-five inch card and ask them to write a one-sentence description of the perfect marriage. After several minutes, take up the cards. Read and discuss them. Ask students, **What does it take to have a marriage like the one you described?** Ask, **Is anything you can do as a teenager to prepare for the kind of marriage you described?**

Ask one or two volunteers to read aloud the stories in section one (pp. 6-7). Lead the group to discuss what was good about Calvin and Sylvia's marriage. Ask them to discuss the problems Katherine experienced. Explain that the Bible study *Living Pure Inside Out* is focused on sexual purity.

STEP 2 Ask students, **How would you define purity?** After students have shared several answers, ask them to form work groups with three or four other students. Give each group a large sheet of paper and markers. Ask groups to read through section two (pp. 8-10) then develop a poster that symbolizes purity. After several minutes, invite groups to share their ideas.

Hang the "Point To Ponder" poster on the wall. Ask, **How is this different from just waiting for marriage to have sexual intercourse?** Direct students to the last paragraph in section two. Group students into same-sex pairs and lead them to discuss their answers on page 10.

STEP 3 Play the video you have recorded from TV. Explain that because of how "messed up" the world is, it is hard to even understand true purity. Lead students to read and complete the material in section three, calling on different youth to read aloud all printed material including Scripture passages. Instruct students to answers the questions in his or her book.

STEP 4 Ask students, **With all the problems in the world these days, is it even possible for a person to lead a sexually pure life?** Explain that while it is not easy, that is exactly what God has called us to do. Ask a volunteer to read 1 Corinthians 6:18-20. Explain that Corinth was a city that was full of sexual immorality, much like our nation is today. Ask, **What did Paul tell the Corinthians to do?** Write their answers on the board. Ask, **What do you think Paul meant when he said that we do not belong to ourselves?** Share with students that Jesus died for our sins. If we trust Him as our Lord and Savior, our lives belong to Him and not ourselves. Ask, **If your life belongs to Christ, what does Jesus have the right to ask of you?** *(He has the right to ask anything of those who are His.)* If you are aware of lost students in your group, give them an opportunity to respond to the gospel.

Read 1 Thessalonians 4:3-4. Ask students, **According to this verse, what is God's will for you?** *(Sexual purity)* Direct students to the checklist on page 17. Ask, **Which of these items would be sexually impure?** *(All of them)* Say, **It really isn't too difficult to know what is impure, is it?**

STEP 5 Read the "True Love Waits" section to the students. Lead the group to pray the final prayer in unison.

FOR DISCIPLENOW
For step 2, video "man on the street interviews" asking people what they think purity is. Play the videos during the evening worship time. For step 4, have small groups create a skit showing God's expectation for sexual purity.

FOR A RETREAT
For step 3, ask the retreat speaker to share the gospel at this point. For step 4, lead youth to do this step on their own in a quiet place reflecting on God's expectations of them personally.

ANSWERS
Section Two: Box 4; hearts, pure, see, God; Box 4
Section Three: Boxes 1, 2, 3, 5; evil, should never be done
Section Four: Jesus' death; Box 2; For us to control our bodies in a way that is holy and honorable; All Boxes

Session 2

Overview: In this session students will discover that it is impossible to be pure in their own strength. Their only hope is Christ living through them.

Before the session:
☐ For step 4: Write the "Point to Ponder" (p. 28) on poster board.

STEP 1 Ask a volunteer to read James' story in section one. Assign students to discussion groups and ask them to discuss the questions following the story. After several minutes, tell students, **A lot of students make commitments to purity and then fail to follow**

through. Even those who don't get involved in premarital sex may get involved in other kinds of sexual impurity. Explain, **You can succeed in sexual purity, but it takes a different approach than the one James used.**

STEP 2 Ask students to form three teams. Assign each team to read and study one of the three problems with living a pure life (pp. 21-23). Direct the teams to report to the group by summarizing and explaining the problem they studied.

STEP 3 Read aloud the story at the beginning of section three, then divide the group into two teams. Direct one team to make up a skit that demonstrates someone who tries harder but still fails. Ask the other team to develop a skit about someone who tries, fails, and then just gives up. Give teams a few minutes to prepare and then call teams to present their skits. (With a large group, you can have four teams using the same two themes for the skits.) Following the skits, read and review all the material, Scriptures, and answers.

STEP 4 Discuss Juan's testimony on page 28. Ask students, **What was wrong with Juan's testimony?** Ask a volunteer to read Galatians 2:19-20. Lead students to discuss what it means to allow Christ to live in you, instead of simply trying to live for Christ. Help students to understand that the Christian life was never supposed to be lived in our own power.

Post the "Point to Ponder" on a focal wall. Ask students to discuss how it relates to Galatians 2:19-20.

Divide the class into three groups and ask each group to examine one of the three hints to walking in the Spirit (pp. 29-32). Ask them to read the Scriptures and descriptions in the section. Lead the group to discuss why that hint is important for walking in God's Spirit.

STEP 5 Read the "True Love Waits" section to the students. Lead the group to pray the final prayer in unison.

FOR DISCIPLENOW

Assign each DiscipleNow group to make a banner with the theme, "I Can't … But He Can." Provide necessary materials. Have groups display their banners at the closing worship service.

FOR A RETREAT

Plan this session to be studied in two different locations. The first part of the study will be of sections one and two. It is the "I Can't" section of the study and should be held in a room decorated in an "I Can't" theme. Making this room a bit gloomy is OK! After sections one and two, move to the new location.

The second part of the study, sections three, four, and five, is to be held in a cheerful room. This is the "He Can" part of the study. Decorate this location in bright, positive colors. Use the contrast in rooms to contrast the difference between our efforts at purity and His efforts as He lives in us.

ANSWERS

Section Two: Boxes 2, 3, 4; Paul wanted to do right; Can't make, do, right; Box 2; We are; Box 1; Box 1

Section Three: Box 3; Jeff and Susan set their minds on God; The message comes from our sinful nature; led, Spirit, God

Section Four: Boxes 1, 2, 3; Word, God; Turn, away, sin; Sam would have confessed and tried to make it right; accountable, believers; Christians can pray together, ask each other questions, confront sin; Barnabas sent for Paul to help him; No, Paul took Silas with him; No, Jesus sent the disciples out two by two

Session 3

Overview: In this session students will discover the dangers of pornography and the way to overcome it.

Before the session:

- ☐ Write the following six phrases on the chalkboard: *Some sins can be kept secret, Some sins are harmless, Pornography is not addictive, Pornography is not really a sin, Pornography is not degrading, Pornography is not the problem.*
- ☐ For step 1: Enlist three guest teachers. The teachers may be other adults or mature youth. Assign each guest to study one of the three reasons there is no secret sin (pp. 35-37), and prepare to lead a discussion of that reason.
- ☐ For step 2: Provide poster board and markers.
- ☐ For step 4: Write the "Point To Ponder" on poster board. Write the five steps to escape on strips of paper.

STEP 1 Begin the session by calling attention to the phrases on the board. Discuss which of these phrases the students believe. You may even take a poll of the group.

Ask a volunteer to read Seth's story and the paragraph that follows it (pp. 34-35). Say, **Our three guest leaders are going to explain to us why there really is no secret sin.** Direct each guest teacher to lead the discussion of his or her point. As each point is discussed, beside where you have written "Some sins can be kept secret" write "God sees," "Others know," and "All will be known."

STEP 2 Divide the group into three teams. Provide each team with poster board and markers. Assign team one to study "Sin damages our fellowship with God" (p.38), team two to study "Sin destroys us" (p. 39), and team three to study "Sin harms our future relationships" (p. 40). Direct each team to create a poster that reflects the truth about the harm done by sin in their assigned study.

After the posters are completed, direct each team to present their poster. As groups share, write beside the phrase "Some sins are harmless" (already on the board) the headings "Sin damages our fellowship with God," "Sin destroys us," and "Sin harms our future relationships." Emphasize that no sin is harmless, especially pornography.

STEP 3 Read the first two paragraphs of "The Trap" then refer to the four lies which are already on the board. Read each lie and have students discuss why each is a lie. After the discussions, read the material in the section, having students answer the questions as you go. As each phrase on the board is exposed as a lie, ask a student to come to the board and draw an X through the phrase.

STEP 4 Hang the "Point to Ponder" poster on a focal wall. Emphasize the truth of the statement. Teach each of the five steps to escape by first attaching the strip containing the step to a focal wall and then reading the material for that step and answering the questions.

When all of the steps are on the focal wall, work with the youth to develop a symbol that represents each step. For example, for "Know the Truth" you could draw the outline of a human head with the word *truth* written inside the head. Draw each of these symbols on the strips containing the steps. Use these symbols as a way to review and learn these steps to escape.

STEP 5 Read the "True Love Waits" section to the students. Lead the group to pray the closing prayer in unison.

FOR DISCIPLENOW

For step 1, make a video showing how there is no secret sin. On the video, show a person whose secret sin is wasting time by secretly playing computer solitaire. In the video, demonstrate the three reasons from the material why no sin is truly secret. After playing the video, use the truth in the video to emphasize how pornography also is not a secret sin. For step 4, ask each student to write a letter to a fictional friend trapped in pornography. In the letter students should include the steps to escape. Read the letters in your group.

FOR A RETREAT

For step 3, invite a person who was trapped in pornography but is now free to come to the retreat and share his or her testimony. For step 5, make a recording on cassette or CD of someone reading section five in the material. Give each youth a cassette or CD and a player and send the youth off to listen in a private place.

ANSWERS

Section One: Nothing can be hidden from God; Cain's face was downcast; Nothing will stay hidden in eternity

Section Two: Boxes 1, 3, 4, 6, 7, 8; Boxes 1, 2, 3

Section Three: David looked at a woman bathing; David may have felt like he couldn't help himself; She was married; David felt he had to have the woman; David, the woman and her husband were all affected by David's sin; Box 2; They are the lamp of the body

Section Four: He always provides a way; Jesus; Box 4

Session 4

Overview: In this session students will learn how to live a pure life.

Before the session:

- ☐ For step 1: Bring a blindfold and masking tape.
- ☐ Write the "Point to Ponder" on poster board and hang it on a wall.
- ☐ For step 2: Provide paper. Enlist a person to share a testimony about dating standards.

☐ For step 3: Provide paper. Write out the five "emotional boundaries" (p. 56) on three-by-five inch cards (one boundary on each card) and have enough blank cards for the maximum number of youth who might be present at this study.

STEP 1 Enlist a volunteer and blindfold him or her. Place a strip of masking tape about one foot long on the floor. Tell students that they are to direct this student to get as close to the strip of masking tape as he or she can without touching it. After they agree that the student is as close as possible, tell the volunteer to take off the blindfold to see where he or she is. Watch the strip of tape closely during the activity. If his or her shoe ever touches the piece of tape, even slightly, disqualify him or her and get another volunteer.

Once students have gotten a volunteer close to the tape without touching it, ask the volunteer how he or she felt about being directed. Ask, **Did you ever get concerned that they would get you too close and you would touch the tape?** Ask, **Would you have felt differently if we had been directing you to the edge of a cliff, trying to get you as close as possible without you falling over the edge?** Ask students to discuss, **How is this activity similar to how some people approach their dating lives?** Students will probably say that some students don't want to have sex before marriage, but they try to edge as close as they can without actually having sex.

Ask a volunteer to read the story on pages 50-51. Direct them to the "Point to Ponder" and lead them to discuss it. Ask them what the difference is between the two questions. Ask students to get a partner. Instruct pairs to read and answer the remainder of page 52.

STEP 2 Ask a volunteer to read Genesis 2:24. Direct students to check the reason for sexual love according to this verse on page 53. Use the material in the next few paragraphs to describe how our bodies naturally want to move toward a one-flesh relationship. Ask volunteers to read the three paragraphs on page 54 beginning with "What does all of this mean practically?" Discuss each paragraph with students. Expect for them to be resistant as this may seem much more restrictive than they have previously been taught. Don't try to force them to accept these principles; suggest that they simply take time to think about them and pray about them.

Ask students to find a quiet place to think and pray. Ask them to respond to the questions at the bottom of the page. Tell them that you will not be asking them to share their answers with others in the group.

STEP 3 Call students back together. Explain that you have been focusing on physical limits in a dating relationship, and those are important. However, help students to understand that they also need to set some emotional limits on a relationship. Read the material on page 55 together and discuss the two descriptions of "falling in love." Ask, **Which is more honoring to God?**

Ask a volunteer to read Philippians 4:6-7. Lead students to discuss what it means for the "peace of Christ" to "guard our hearts." Ask, **Why do you think our hearts need guarding?** Explain that some students are devastated by a break-up with a boyfriend or girlfriend. While it is never fun to experience rejection, some students have invested so much in a relationship that they don't think they can go on. Some have even turned to suicide. Explain that we will experience pain in life, but God wants to guard our hearts from the pain of emotional attachments that are made too early in a relationship.

Shuffle the cards with the five emotional boundaries written on them into the stack of blank cards, so there is one card for each student with all but five cards blank. Pass the cards out with the writing side down. Call on the students who received the written boundaries to read their card. Ask the group if they agree with this boundary, and why. Explain that these cards are some suggestions for setting emotional boundaries, but there may be other emotional boundaries we should set in dating relationships. Explain that the intention of having emotional boundaries is to, by faith, allow God to guard your heart.

STEP 4 Ask a volunteer to read the story of Carl on page 57 and lead students to respond to the questions following the story. Ask a volunteer to read Psalm 119: 9 and ask students to check the correct response on page 58. Explain, **While the Bible never talks about dating like we practice in America, it does give some clear standards of what relationships between men and women should be like.**

Divide the group into four small groups. Assign each group one of the four standards (pp. 58-61). Direct them to read their section of study and then develop a short skit illustrating their standard. Allow each group to present their skit. Then lead students to look at Scriptures included in that section of the material and discuss why that standard is important and how they can live out that standard in their lives.

Ask a student to read Galatians 5:16. Lead students to discuss the four suggestions for walking in the Spirit (pp. 62-63). Ask volunteers to read the material under each suggestion as you discuss them.

STEP 5 Read the "True Love Waits" section to the students. Lead the group to pray the closing prayer in unison.

FOR DISCIPLENOW

For steps 2-3, develop a collage on the kitchen table. Collect items representative of the physical and emotional aspects of relationships. Draw a boundary on a piece of poster board. Place some items in bounds and some items out of bounds based on this study.

FOR A RETREAT

For step 4, do a mock dating game or a role-play activity in which the girl chooses her date based on the four standards. For step 5, send the youth off to be by themselves to consider praying the closing prayer on their own. Challenge youth to seriously consider if this is the desire of their heart.

ANSWERS

Section Two: Box 2

Section Three: The second way of falling in love honors God; Jesus is in charge of guarding our hearts

Section Four: Carl's standards were self-centered instead of God-centered; God should set the standards for a Christian's dating life; Box 1; Box 2; Box 2; Box 4; Demas gave up while Peter and Paul didn't

Session 5

Overview: In this session students will make a commitment to remain sexually pure as God leads.

Before the session:

- ☐ For step 1: Provide poster board and markers.
- ☐ For step 2: Provide paper. Write the "Point to Ponder" on poster board.
- ☐ For step 3: Make copies of the True or False Test on page 91-92.
- ☐ For step 4: Make poster strips with the headings: *Identify the commitment, Privately affirm the commitment in your spirit, Make your commitment public.* Provide enough True Love Waits Commitment Cards (ISBN 0-6330-8888-9) for each student.

STEP 1 Divide the group into teams of five or six and give each team a piece of poster board and markers. Assign each team to read section one and make a poster that shows how a person can be successful in making a commitment to sexual purity. After the teams finish their posters, lead the groups to display them around the room.

STEP 2 Give students a piece of paper and instruct them to write an unsigned response about a time when they didn't keep a commitment. Collect the unsigned papers and read the responses to the group. Comment that we all know the frustration of making a commitment and not being able to keep it. Explain, **The best way to keep a commitment is to start by making the commitment in faith.**

Lead the group to study section two. When you finish studying the section, post the "Point to Ponder" on a focal wall. Explain that this statement explains the hope we have for making a True Love Waits commitment to purity and actually keeping the commitment.

STEP 3 Lead students to study section three. At the end of the study of this section, give each student a copy of the following True or False Test. Explain that students are to answer the questions based on the study they have just finished.

THE CHARACTERISTICS OF A COMMITMENT TRUE OR FALSE TEST

___ **1. A commitment should be specific in nature, not general.**

___ **2. When making a commitment to purity, you should identify specific standards and boundaries God has brought to your life.**

___ **3. Making a secret commitment to purity is what True Love Waits is all about.**

___ **4. Jesus said if we are shy, it is OK to keep our commitment a secret.**

___ **5. If you make a commitment under pressure from others, just be thankful your friends care if you are sexually pure or not.**

___ **6. We should all try to pressure our friends to sign a pledge card.**

___ **7. If you go through this study and don't make a commitment, you are no friend of God's.**

After the test, review the answers and discuss the questions. *(Answers: 1. T; 2. T; 3. F; 4. F; 5. F; 6. F; 7. F)*

STEP 4 Lead students to study through section four. As you study each step, hang the poster strip with the step written on it on a focal wall. When you arrive at "Make your commitment public," give each student a True Love Waits Commitment Card. Tell students who are ready to make this commitment to sign the card. Call upon students who signed a commitment card to stand up and tell the group what their True Love Waits commitment means to them. You may also want to have a worship service dedicated to True Love Waits where students make their commitment public in front of the church body. Encourage students to take their cards home and share with their parents about the commitment they made. Tell them to encourage their parents to sign a pledge to purity on the back of the card.

STEP 5 Conclude the study by reading the "True Love Waits" section to the students. Lead the group to pray the closing prayer in unison.

FOR DISCIPLENOW

If you have a commitment worship time at DiscipleNow, make the signing of the commitment cards the focus of the commitment time. Invite parents to come to this service and give them an opportunity to sign the card with their teenager.

FOR A RETREAT

For step 2, lead youth to develop a skit showing an example of how people fail to keep a commitment. For step 4, build an outdoor altar where you can lay their commitment cards.

ANSWERS

Section Two: Boxes 2, 3; with you, protect you, bring you safely back, be with you constantly; Jesus went to Zacchaeus' house; Zacchaeus gave half his possessions to the poor, he would pay back four times anyone he had cheated; Box 1; God will begin any commitment you make; Trust God to complete any commitment you make to Him

Section Three: Boxes 3, 5; Aaron said exactly what he was going to do and when he was going to do it; Boxes 2, 4; Jesus could see that the Holy Spirit was working on Zacchaeus; Boxes 1, 3, 5, 7; Other guys probably didn't think Danny was serious; Jesus will be ashamed of them when He comes in glory; refrain, making, vow, not, guilty

Section Four: asked; Boxes 1, 2, 3

TRUE LOVE WAITS COMMITMENT

Believing that true love waits, I make a commitment to God, myself, my family, my friends, my future mate, and my future children to a lifetime of purity including sexual abstinence from this day until the day I enter a biblical marriage relationship.

Signed ______________________________ **Date** __________

True Love Waits Goes Home also includes a challenge to parents of teens (or other significant adults in their lives) to sign a commitment to sexual purity. When parents make a similar commitment to their teens, God can develop purity in the entire home and family. Here is the commitment for parents and significant adults:

Believing that true love is pure, I join ____________________ (insert student's name) in committing to a lifestyle of purity. I make a commitment to God, myself, my family, and my community of faith to abstain from pornography, impure touching and conversations, and sex outside a biblical marriage relationship from this day forward.

Signed ______________________________ **Date** __________

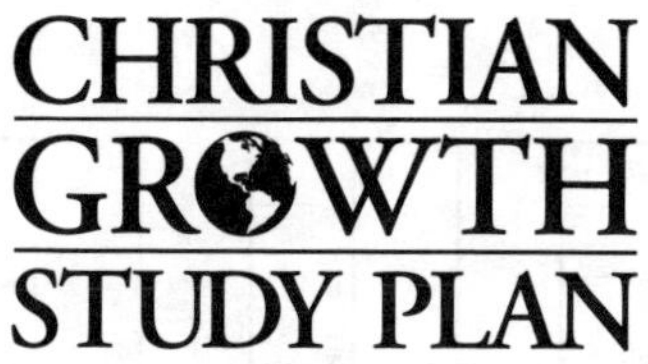

In the **Christian Growth Study Plan (formerly Church Study Course),** this book *Living Pure Inside Out* is a resource for course credit in the subject area "Ethics" of the Christian Growth category of plans. To receive credit, read the book, complete the learning activities, show your work to your pastor, a staff member or church leader, then complete the following information. This page may be duplicated. Send the completed page to:

Christian Growth Study Plan
One LifeWay Plaza • Nashville, TN 37234-0117
FAX: (615)251-5067 • Email: cgspnet@lifeway.com

For information about the Christian Growth Study Plan, refer to the Christian Growth Study Plan Catalog. It is located online at www.lifeway.com/cgsp. If you do not have access to the Internet, contact the Christian Growth Study Plan office (1.800.968.5519) for the specific plan you need for your ministry.

Living Pure Inside Out CG-0803

PARTICIPANT INFORMATION

Social Security Number (USA ONLY-optional)	Personal CGSP Number*	Date of Birth (MONTH, DAY, YEAR)
– –	– –	– –

Name (First, Middle, Last)	Home Phone
	– –

Address (Street, Route, or P.O. Box)	City, State, or Province	Zip/Postal Code

CHURCH INFORMATION

Church Name		
Address (Street, Route, or P.O. Box)	City, State, or Province	Zip/Postal Code

CHANGE REQUEST ONLY

☐ Former Name		
☐ Former Address	City, State, or Province	Zip/Postal Code
☐ Former Church	City, State, or Province	Zip/Postal Code

Signature of Pastor, Conference Leader, or Other Church Leader	Date

*New participants are requested but not required to give SS# and date of birth. Existing participants, please give CGSP# when using SS# for the first time. Thereafter, only one ID# is required. **Mail to:** Christian Growth Study Plan, One LifeWay Plaza, Nashville, TN 37234-0117. Fax: (615)251-5067.

Rev. 10-01